MOVING THE HOUSING MARKET

Moving the Housing Market

Council estates, social change and privatization

RAY FORREST
University of Bristol

ALAN MURIE
Heriot-Watt University, Edinburgh

Avebury
Aldershot · Brookfield USA · Hong Kong · Singapore · Sydney

Published by
Avebury
Gower Publishing Company Limited
Gower House
Croft Road
Aldershot
Hants GU11 3HR
England

Gower Publishing Company
Old Post Road
Brookfield
Vermont 05036
USA

British Library Cataloguing in Publication Data
Forrest, Ray
Moving the housing market : council estates, social change and privatization.
1. Great Britain. Housing market
I. Title II. Murie, Alan 1946-
363.50941

ISBN 1-85628-046-2

Printed and Bound in Great Britain by
Athenaeum Press Ltd., Newcastle upon Tyne.

Contents

List of tables

List of figures

1 Introduction

We have now had a decade of Thatcherism. Various accounts and assessments have appeared which have analysed the successes and failures and compared rhetoric and reality. Debates continue as to whether the ideological shifts have been profound or illusory. In any account of the Thatcher years, privatization must be a prominent feature. And the decline of council housing through sales and dwindling new investment remains one of the most overt consequences of a changed political environment for welfare provision. Whatever one's perspective on the merits or otherwise of selling council houses it is undeniable that the last decade has seen a marked change in patterns of housing provision and in attitudes towards the delivery of housing services. In Britain, a million and a half council houses have been transferred to the private sector and the period up until the next general election is likely to see a substantial further transfer. Levels of new council building will continue to be very low and the sector will age and decline in size. Those who remain in the public rented sector, whether under local authority or housing association control, are likely to face a regime of rising rents and rent differentials linked to property values. There is no indication that the spiral of decline for council housing will ease or that the encouragements and incentives for those who can and want to 'exit' from the sector will in any way diminish. Indeed, a 1989 survey of attitudes to housing and tenure preferences found a significant increase in interest among council tenants in the purchase of their dwelling. Some 40 per cent expressed an interest in buying and 22 per cent thought they were likely to do so (Building Societies Association, 1989). Previous surveys had shown that typically around 15 per cent of tenants were likely to buy (Forrest and

Murie, 1988a, p. 128). Part of this increased interest in council house purchase must be attributable to the factors referred to above as well as more generous discounts and less restrictive conditions on purchase.

By the early 1990s less than 20 per cent of households are likely to remain in the public sector in England. Access to housing to rent or purchase will be dominated by market processes. Arguably, however, the effects of the bureaucratic allocation of housing will not be removed until former council dwellings enter the housing market on resale. They will then become part of the general pool of houses to buy or rent, distinguishable perhaps by design and locational features but otherwise with no separate, predetermined role to play in housing provision. Who will buy or rent former council houses? Will former council dwellings continue to provide housing for relatively low income groups? Will there be significant spatial variations depending on local tenure structures and property values? Will former council homes be better maintained after privatization? This book is concerned with these and other related issues. It reports the results of original research designed to address these questions.

A considerable amount of information already exists about the sale of council dwellings in terms of the financial and fiscal impacts, the characteristics of purchasers, the kinds of dwellings sold and the geography of privatization (for a general assessment see Forrest and Murie, 1988a). Evidence remains scant, however, on the longer term consequences and the ways in which former council homes are incorporated into the market. This is understandable, given that the vast majority of sales have occurred since 1980 under the Right to Buy and it is only in the 1990s that sufficient resales will begin to occur for this aspect to be explored. Whereas research on council house sales has tended to focus on the consequences of council house sales for the council housing which remains (for example, in terms of residualization) there are equally important questions to be asked of the people and dwellings which have left the public sector. There is also a need to move beyond housing policy detail and discussion of the distributional consequences of the sale of council houses.

This book is concerned with the longer term impact of council house sales on the social structure of neighbourhoods and with aspects of social change on council estates. The existing literature on social change and tenure conversion in Britain and in other countries has focused on the conversion of privately rented properties and on gentrification and social change following this. No doubt this has been a key aspect of social and neighbourhood change in the post-war period. But in the 1980s it has been change from council housing to home ownership which has become the most common form of tenure conversion in Britain. The consequence of this, as with the earlier phase of tenure conversion, is not some immediate neighbourhood social change. However, changing ownership and processes of access will affect who moves in when properties change hands. Moving the market to embrace council housing neighbourhoods means changing the processes to be negotiated by people seeking housing there. Whether or not that process significantly alters the social role and composition of those neighbourhoods is an empirical question. This study provides the first detailed evidence on this issue.

The Research

Council house sales have a history which precedes the Thatcher administration by a considerable number of years. For this reason we have been able to sample council dwellings sold between 1968 and 1973 under the discretionary policies pursued by Birmingham City Council, and the Greater London Council in the London Boroughs of Barking and Havering. The core of the research involved carrying out face to face interviews with the principal earner of the household or their partner in 416 former council owned dwellings. The 416 properties were split evenly between estates in London and Birmingham. The research design was influenced significantly by the existence of a survey of council house purchasers carried out in 1973 (Murie, 1975). This provided the sampling frame in Birmingham and dictated the time period (1968-1973) for the London sample. The interviews were carried out by a market research agency in September and October 1988. Further work and analysis was carried out subsequently in an attempt to trace and interview households who had moved since purchasing their council dwelling. Additionally, a house condition survey was undertaken in Birmingham to compare sold dwellings with similar properties remaining in the council sector.

The samples in London and Birmingham are not strictly comparable. The original Birmingham survey was spread over a wide geographical area. For London, in order to facilitate sampling and to control for dwelling quality, the sample was chosen from two estates, Becontree in Dagenham and Harold Hill in Romford. Both estates are of good quality council houses. They represent some of the better examples of public sector provision. The Becontree estate opened in 1921 and was known at one time as the largest municipal housing estate in the world. It was working class housing of the 'Fordist' regime in the truest sense of the word given its adjacency to the Ford factory, at that time the largest car plant outside the United States. By 1945 the Becontree estate had a total of 14,724 dwellings (GLC, 1976, p. 32). Whilst its beginnings as a 'garden city' cottage estate were eroded by the growing financial restrictions of the 1920s it contains nevertheless some substantial and high quality public sector dwellings. The Harold Hill estate is more recent in origin having opened in 1948. It is overwhelmingly an estate of houses rather than flats. Out of some 4,500 dwellings, over two-thirds are houses.

The original sample in Birmingham was not linked to particular housing estates but scattered across a large area of the city. Previous research in the city has established the characteristics of the dwellings sold between 1968 and 1973 as typically the better located, better quality, on the more popular outer suburban estates. Almost three-quarters of dwellings in the Birmingham sample were three bedroomed semi detached or terraced. There were no acquired dwellings, no flats and no one bedroomed dwellings. In that period (1968-73) such properties were explicitly excluded from the sales policy (Forrest and Murie, 1976; Murie, 1975). Purposely, therefore, we are examining in this study some of the best examples of working class housing provided by the state. These were the homes fit for the heroes of two world wars. And those tenants who were the beneficiaries of the more generous phases of state building were also the subsequent principal beneficiaries of council house sales. It is this group of tenants which is the main focus of this book. What happened to them after they bought their houses? How many are still living there? Are there notable differences between areas which have experienced high levels of house price inflation, such as London, and areas where gains have potentially been more modest? What attitudes do the original purchasers now hold towards public housing and home ownership? Have their political orientations changed as they have progressed through home ownership? On resale, who has moved into these properties and in what ways do they differ from current tenants and the original purchasers? How have the properties fared in the private sector as regards repair and maintenance?

The Structure of the Book

The book is divided into six main chapters. In the chapter which follows, the focus is on the original sitting tenant purchasers who have remained in the same dwellings. The next chapter (Chapter 3), describes the incomers who bought the dwellings on resale and builds on the work carried out on this issue in Birmingham in 1978 (Forrest, 1980). Chapter 4 deals with the more difficult questions around the households who have moved from those dwellings. In this chapter there is also some discussion of the methodological difficulties involved in tracing households. Chapter 5 focuses on the properties rather than the people and reports on a house condition survey carried out on our behalf in Birmingham. Results of this survey of sold dwellings are compared with a recent survey of tenanted properties carried out by the council. Chapter 6 uses the detailed evidence from this research to explore a number of general debates regarding attitudes towards housing tenure. The final chapter is more broad-ranging in style and content. It draws out the key issues and findings from the previous chapters and reflects on their implications for both policy and theoretical debates in housing.

The research on which this book is based was funded by the Joseph Rowntree Memorial Trust.

2 The long term residents – purchasers who stay put

There is now a substantial literature on council house sales which details the characteristics of purchasers and properties which have been sold. This presents a picture of tenure change but initially does not involve social change. Purchases of council homes by sitting tenants do not change the social composition of areas. Two propositions however arise in relation to this. First, over time, tenant purchaser households will dissolve or move. Second, there is a view that changing tenure status - becoming a home owner - affects the interests and attitudes of households. The same households may change their allegiances and identities.

A considerable amount of speculation has arisen about the rate at which council house purchasers move. This has mostly been linked with a discussion of the loss of relets - the effect that the sale of council houses has on reducing the supply of properties becoming available for letting by the council. Discussion of social change associated with resales should be couched in different terms. Rather than being concerned with the rate at which people would have moved had they remained tenants, issues of social change relate to actual movement by owner occupiers. This may involve a greater rate of movement because home ownership may create greater scope for some households to move. Any vacancies created by this movement will be filled through a market process and not bureaucratic allocation. Who moves into former council houses through this process is the subject of the next chapter. This chapter is concerned with initial questions about what proportion of households still live in the dwellings they purchased as sitting tenants and about their attitudes.

Household Characteristics

One of the key questions relating to social change in council estates affected by privatization is how far tenure change has led to population change. How many people are still living in the dwellings they bought from their council in the 1968-1973 period? In London, of the 197 households interviewed in this study, 56 per cent were the original purchasers (or in some cases the surviving spouse). In Birmingham the proportion was slightly higher at 61 per cent. Taking the sample as a whole, well over half the households had not moved since purchasing between fifteen and twenty years ago. Whether or not this level of turnover is surprising relative to general levels of residential mobility is difficult to ascertain. Appropriate comparisons would be with older, established working class home owners who undoubtedly have a lower mobility rate than home owners in general and younger, first time buyers in particular, or with council tenants with similar age and class characteristics. It is worth reminding ourselves that in the earlier study of council house purchasers in Birmingham (Murie, 1975), the typical purchaser household was 'a long established tenant, ... in middle age with a fairly large family growing up. He is earning above average wages, usually in a skilled manual occupation' (p. 103).

Over fifteen years on from that survey we are therefore dealing with a relatively elderly group of former tenants. Table 1 shows that the proportion of original purchaser households aged 60 or over was 49 per cent in London and 65 per cent in Birmingham. Among other things this might indicate that early purchasers in London were slightly younger. This might reflect a different demographic structure among London's council tenants. However, the sampling in London was carried out on only two estates and the Birmingham sample may be more representative.

For mobility and turnover, it is instructive to look back on the 1973 survey in Birmingham and responses to the questions on moving intentions. Asked if 'they might move from this house' only 23 per cent gave a positive response. And of that 23 per cent less than half thought they would move within ten years (p. 126). Judged against those figures the turnover rate is not at all surprising. What is perhaps more surprising is the degree of consistency between the two surveys in Birmingham. Responses to hypothetical questions about moving intentions over a long timescale are generally regarded as no more than illustrative and requiring extreme caution in interpretation. Such caveats remain. In this case, however, it could have been predicted that of the original Birmingham sample some two-thirds of households would still be there after ten years. The actual figure after fifteen years was 61 per cent.

To what extent was this pattern of turnover a consequence of constraint rather than choice? A higher rate of movement might for example be expected as households enter or near retirement. Certainly, as the households in this sample age, some acceleration of turnover is inevitable through mortality, ill health, moves to specialist sheltered accommodation and so on. However, at the time of the survey less than 6 per cent of the non-moving households in both Birmingham and London had ever tried to move. Of those who had, only two mentioned difficulties with selling the house as the reason for not moving. Indeed, there was no indication that movement had been inhibited for any negative reasons. Much more likely is the simple fact that we are dealing with a mature and locally sedimented group of households with strong attachments to their neighbourhood. In this context, it should be borne in mind that of the original Birmingham purchasers, 45 per cent had moved into the dwellings they purchased before 1960 (Murie, 1975, p. 110).

Few of the original purchasers anticipated moving in the next few years. Some 75 per cent of households in both Birmingham and London expected to remain where they were living for the foreseeable future. For those contemplating moving, life cycle considerations associated with ageing were the primary reason. Of those who gave reasons, moving to a smaller house or flat was the most commonly cited. It should be stressed that in this chapter we are examining a sub-group of original tenant purchasers, namely those who had stayed. Our knowledge of those who moved on remains scanty and we cannot draw any conclusions about purchasers in general from the data presented here. Some limited evidence about those who moved on is presented in Chapter 4.

Some of the other data presented in Table 2.1 deserve some brief comment. They provide a general profile of the sample in terms of family life cycle stage, occupational class and economic circumstances. Broadly, they conform to the image of purchasing households established across a number of surveys (e.g. Murie, 1975; Forrest and Murie, 1984; Sewel et al., 1984; Foulis, 1985; Kerr, 1988). Differences between the age profiles of the samples are reflected in the higher proportions of households in London who fall into the non-elderly couple category and who have more than one worker in full time employment. As regards household type they are typically large adult households or two person households with at least one person aged 60 or above. They are overwhelmingly in the skilled or semi-skilled manual occupation categories. Most of them were born and brought up in their respective towns and many of their children continue to live nearby. On this last point, the apparent difference between the London and Birmingham groups should be treated with some caution. Respondents were allowed to interpret neighbourhood according to their own perceptions. In spatial terms a Birmingham neighbourhood may be rather smaller than a London one. All we can say is that a higher proportion of the London purchasers have children living in what they regard as the same neighbourhood.

Table 2.1
The purchasers of council houses between 1968 and 1973: selected characteristics

	London households	Birmingham households
	110	134
Sample number	%	%
Age of respondent		
25-44	7	2
45-59	42	30
60-74	45	56
75+	4	9
Not known	2	4
Household type	%	%
1 non-elderly adult	3	4
2 non-elderly adults	21	12
Households with children	6	3
Large adult household	34	30
Single elderly person	6	16
Two adults (at least one elderly)	29	31
Not known	2	4
Economic household type	%	%
One worker FT/no retired	12	10
One worker FT/at least one retired	8	13
More than one worker (FT/PT)/no retired	41	23
More than one worker (FT/PT)/at least one retired	4	7
No worker (or just 1 PT)/no retired	4	9
No worker (or just 1 PT)/at least one retired	30	38
Not known	2	-
Social class	%	%
Professional	-	-
Managerial	5	1
Junior white collar	23	21
Skilled manual	46	41
Semi-skilled manual	25	26
Unskilled manual	1	7
Not known	1	3

Table 2.1 (continued)

	London households	Birmingham households
	110	134
	%	%
Birthplace of respondent		
London/Birmingham	81	73
Elsewhere in UK	12	17
Outside UK	5	8
Not known	2	1
Children living away from home	%	%
Living in same neighbourhood as parents	43	23
Elsewhere in London/Birmingham	7	34
In same region (i.e. SE, W. Midlands)	33	16
Elsewhere	14	24
Not known	3	2

From what we know of previous research on households who purchased their dwellings from the council in the late 1960s and early 1970s, none of this is particularly surprising. Generally, such households were the relatively affluent and secure members of the local working class. But how did they fare in the recession of the late 1970s and early 1980s which had particularly devastating effects in the larger conurbations including London and Birmingham? Table 2.2 provides some information on this aspect and confirms the picture of relative job security. Of respondents and partners, no-one was unemployed throughout the period. Very few were in and out of employment or in less secure employment. Overall, the picture is one of stability with few dramatic positive or negative changes. For this group at least, house purchase was not paralleled by any notably enhanced occupational position. Neither was the equity acquired through home ownership used to support any substantial shift into self-employment.

The long term residents - tenants who bought but have stayed - are not a deprived or disadvantaged group whose income or financial circumstances would have prevented moving or whose actions demonstrate a desire to move which they have not been able to fulfil. They are households with strong attachments to their dwelling and its locality. They did not buy in order to move geographically or to move up some housing ladder. Rather they were confirming existing satisfaction with their home. And their subsequent behaviour has restated this. Nevertheless their attitudes towards tenure and their political behaviour could have changed. It is these issues which are addressed in the rest of this chapter.

Table 2.2
Employment history since purchase

	London		Birmingham	
Sample Number	Resp.	Spouse	Resp.	Spouse
	110	74	134	59
	%	%	%	%
In work, same kind of job	44	42	49	47
In work, different kind of job	11	18	14	15
In work, promoted	10	3	5	2
In work, job less secure	0	4	1	0
In and out of work	0	4	2	2
Became self-employed	4	1	1	0
Unemployed throughout	0	0	0	0
Housewife in FT employment	5	3	7	12
Housewife in PT employment	16	8	3	7
Housewife not in paid employment	13	12	14	17
Other/Don't know	4	7	4	0

Attitudes towards Tenure

In recent years, in the context of general debates about privatization and privatism, an extensive discussion has developed around the social relations of housing tenure. Without rehearsing the detail and complexity of these debates (see, for example, Gray, 1982; Forrest, 1983; Pratt, 1982; Saunders and Harris, 1988; Forrest and Murie, 1988) an increasingly prominent feature is the view of state housing as being intrinsically and overwhelmingly unpopular. This is perhaps most clearly expressed by Saunders and Harris:

> What all this amounts to is that there is a high degree of dissatisfaction among tenants, and it is this rather than any ideological factor which lies at the root of their strong but often frustrated desire to 'exit' from the state sector. (p. 15)

This is not the place to enter into a detailed critique of this position. It is worth noting in passing, however, that there is a substantial body of evidence on council house purchase which would suggest that economic push and pull factors (i.e. discounts, rising rents) are important factors in decisions to purchase. Also, evidence on those who purchased in the earlier phases of sales (Murie, 1975) establishes that a substantial number could have afforded to buy elsewhere in the private market. Evidently, the desire to exit was not powerful enough to move house. In high house price areas such as London there are additional factors. Access to home ownership has been effectively denied to a larger proportion of working class households through affordability problems. Substantial discounts on council houses may have been the only route into home ownership.

Frustration in this context, and the desire to purchase council dwellings, might be more appropriately located in the unequal competition for residential space rather than linked to the intolerable paternalism and inefficient management of state housing.

The research evidence reported in this book, in this chapter and in Chapter 4, suggests that sitting tenant purchasers had positive attitudes to the home prior to buying and this is apparent from previous studies (Murie, 1975). Nonetheless, the question of how far becoming an owner intensifies 'privatism' or 'home-centredness' remains relevant. Does becoming a home owner create a different identity with the home and what attitudes are held towards housing tenure?

More recently Saunders (1990) has not referred so strongly to a desire to exit. However he still emphasizes the negative views held by many tenants.

> Many council tenants are in this sense reluctant consumers, for we have already seen that three in every four would prefer to be buying their home. It is not, therefore, surprising that over four in ten of them can think of nothing positive to say about their situation. (p. 90)

Saunders acknowledges that problems lay 'not so much in the bricks and mortar as in the social organization of the tenure' and 'lack of control' tenants had over their homes (p. 91) and that some of the

> ... dissatisfaction can be explained as a response to a decline in the quality of the public housing service as a result of government expenditure cuts and limits on local government budgets .... But when all that has been said, the overwhelming impression remains that the basic problem is a crippling and frustrating sense of powerlessness felt by many tenants. Many of those to whom we spoke felt unable to do anything when the clerks in the office ignored them or when the workers who came to their homes did a bodged job, and it was this inability to control factors affecting their own domestic environment which drove so many of them to anger, fatalism, or despair. (p. 94)

Finally, Saunders goes on to argue that

> ... the meanings which people derive from and invest in their homes may be influenced by whether or not they own them. It seems from the tenants' answers that people may find it difficult to establish a sense of belonging in a house which they do not own. This does not mean that tenants suffer acute anomie and lack any sense of belonging at all, but rather that they find such an identity in other ways. Because the house is not personal to them, they emphasize family and neighbours when they think of home. (p. 273)

Saunders refers specifically to council house purchasers in this context:

> The council house purchasers are an interesting group in this respect, for 41 of the 45 of them in the sample are still living in the same house which they previously rented from the local authority. Their family circumstances have not changed, their neighbourhood has not changed, and the house they are living in is still the same house (although many of them have altered its appearance in various ways), yet their orientation to home is dramatically different from that of most of the tenants around them.

Saunders states

> Whether it is that people with a different orientation to home apply to buy their houses, or whether it is the act of purchase which changes the way they think about their homes, is difficult to judge. Probably both factors operate together.

But somewhat contradictorily he goes on to state

> What is clear, however, is that owners are more likely than tenants to express a sense of self and belonging through their houses, *and that this difference is related to ownership rather than to the nature of the housing itself.* (Our emphasis)

In this study, we are examining a group of households who have had substantial experience of both home ownership and council housing in the same dwelling. It therefore provides an unusual opportunity to examine attitudes towards different forms of provision without the complications associated with changes in dwelling type, location and general environment. Table 2.3 summarizes a number of matched questions about council housing and home ownership. Asking people to recall past circumstances involves a number of problems relating for example to selective memory and post hoc rationalization. There is however no reason to believe that households in this sample will have consistently positive or negative bias in their recollections of council housing. Some commentators might point out that the circumstances of council tenants in the 1950s and 1960s were rather different and that responses may be quite dissimilar from tenants purchasing under the Right to Buy. If so, that simply underlines the contingent rather than intrinsic attributes of forms of housing provision. Moreover, this rather specific set of questions addressed to a group of households with similar housing histories may be more robust and reliable than the often vague, ahistorical and uncontextualized questions on tenure preferences common in social surveys.

Table 2.3 sets out respondents' feelings of satisfaction or dissatisfaction across a range of issues such as housing costs, mobility, repairs and maintenance and personal freedom. One point is immediately striking. Home ownership scores highly on all counts. This is true even on issues such as housing costs and 'security if circumstances changed' where a more muted response might have been expected from working class owners. It should be borne in mind, however, that a high proportion of respondents are outright owners (36 per cent in London and 74 per cent in Birmingham) and many have been so for some time. This fact, combined with the discounted price originally paid, sets this group of households into a relatively privileged position among working class owners. Certainly, many of them would have been unaffected by the recent rise in mortgage interest rates. Moreover, many of them are net savers with building societies or banks. Nevertheless, the high level of contentment with home ownership is clear and unequivocal. What is perhaps ambiguous is the relationship between their past experience as council tenants and their current state of wellbeing as home owners. As we have argued elsewhere, attitudes towards forms of housing provision and interpretations of current circumstances are shaped in critical ways by housing experiences over a lifetime (Forrest and Murie, 1987). In other words, people's attitudes towards council housing or home ownership are not formed in a tenurial vacuum where previous experiences of other forms of provision play no part. To have entered home ownership through sitting tenant purchase of a council house is a qualitatively different experience from purchasing a dwelling house on departure from the parental, owner occupied home.

A number of important points emerge from questions about attitudes towards public housing. People are most dissatisfied with aspects of mobility, repairs and maintenance and the lack of freedom to do what they want with the property. Also, former tenants do not regard council housing as being a more secure option if circumstances change. Home ownership scores notably higher on this count. Again this may be influenced by the relatively secure employment situation of this group combined with low housing costs. For example, only three households said they had ever experienced serious problems with meeting their mortgage payments. Issues such as repossession or eviction may not be seen as potential problems by a group of households with little or no mortgage costs and with substantial housing equity. There are also notable differences between the London and Birmingham groups. Birmingham households generally look back on their experiences as tenants with a greater degree of dissatisfaction. Nonetheless, the vast majority express satisfaction with their council as a landlord. And on issues of housing quality and housing costs there is little to choose between the tenures. Moreover, well over two-thirds of former tenants had positive feelings that their rented house was their own home. Predictably, this feeling is almost universal under home ownership. Nevertheless, the fact that over 70 per cent of our sample were satisfied that as council tenants their house was their own is hardly consistent with a view of alienated serfdom as the common experience of tenants, or the claim that people can only really be at home in an owner occupied house (Saunders, 1986, p. 329). One response to this observation would be that we are dealing here with a very peculiar sample of people who have lived in the same house for many years. Perhaps responses would be very different among former tenants who had moved to become home owners. Moreover, households in this group have generally had a very positive experience of public housing. They lived in high quality estates through a period of low (or reasonable?) rents.

Once again, however, such arguments and qualifications merely underline the contingent nature of housing experiences in any tenure and caution against constructing overpolarized images of public housing and home ownership. If for a moment we can refer simply to a pro home ownership and a pro public housing camp then these data would give comfort to both. Entry to home ownership raises levels of satisfaction across a range of factors. Equally, however, on some measures there is no difference or the differences are not as great as some theoretical formulations would have us believe. Moreover, those aspects of public housing where there are the lowest levels of satisfaction are not necessary and inevitable features of social housing.

Table 2.3
The experience of council housing and home ownership: council house purchasers 1968-1973 (Percentages across)
N = 110 (London), 134 (Birmingham)

	Satisfied		Neither satisfied nor dissatisfied		Dissatisfied		Can't remember/ No opinion	
	Council housing	Home ownership	Council housing	Home ownership	Council housing	Home ownership	Council housing	Home ownership
The council as landlord								
London	85	-	7	-	3	-	5	-
Birmingham	79	-	6	-	12	-	2	-
Quality of the accommodation								
London	82	95	7	3	9	2	2	1
Birmingham	91	87	1	1	4	10	3	2
Getting repairs/maintenance done								
London	64	80	8	8	19	5	9	7
Birmingham	56	87	10	1	29	11	5	1
Feeling it was your own home								
London	71	96	10	3	11	1	8	-
Birmingham	72	98	7	-	16	1	4	1
Rent levels/mortgage costs								
London	80	84	5	5	5	3	9	8
Birmingham	75	81	7	4	14	-	4	16
Ability to move								
London	49	73	13	5	12	6	26	15
Birmingham	40	81	7	10	32	5	22	4
Freedom to do what you want with property								
London	45	93	19	1	25	5	10	2
Birmingham	46	94	6	2	43	3	5	1
Security if circumstances change								
London	53	91	14	4	11	2	23	4
Birmingham	51	93	10	1	31	1	8	4

Note: Because of rounding percentages may not total 100.

Privatization, Privatism and Conservatism

There is an image of the council house purchaser as someone who, having thrown off the chains of stifling, paternalistic collectivism, proceeds to shift political allegiance and embark on a privatized lifestyle. This might include voting Conservative rather than Labour, opting for private medical insurance or private education and buying stocks and shares. How far do this early group of council house purchasers conform to this image? In the survey a number of questions were asked about voting behaviour, investments and attitudes towards the local council and council services. It should be stressed that no causal connection is necessarily inferred between, say, buying a council house and buying shares in British Telecom (although such inferences are often drawn in this context). As Heath et al. (1985) point out:

> It is one thing to show an *association* between housing and attitudes towards income redistribution. It is another to demonstrate a *causal* connection. The assumption that the spread of home ownership has political significance depends on the existence of a causal connection. It has never been properly demonstrated. (p. 48)

The respondents in this survey were asked how they had voted over the past twenty years or so. The results are given in Table 2.4. Of those who were committed clearly to one party or another, the Labour Party had the highest level of support. This was, however, rather less marked among Birmingham purchasers, almost a third of whom stated that they had always voted Conservative. Whilst a considerable number did not vote, did not reply or voted for several parties, there was a clear shift towards the Conservative Party. Indeed, the figures overall suggest that the Conservatives could have the support of the majority of the households in the Birmingham sample. How do these data compare with more general psephological analyses? Heath et al. (1985) reviewed previous findings and conducted their own analysis of the 1983 election results. Among other things, they examined the relationship between housing and political allegiance. In 1983, whereas 53 per cent of home owners supported the Conservative Party, this was true of only 23 per cent of council tenants. More specifically, among working class home owners, 39 per cent were Conservative voters (pp. 45-46). Direct comparisons with our sample are not possible but the figures suggest that our purchaser households are more likely to vote Conservative than council tenants in general and less likely to compared with working class home owners. This would not be surprising given arguments that the local milieu is a significant influence on political attitudes (see, for example, Garrahan, 1977; Johnston, 1987). Here we have a group of households who have changed tenure but have remained in residential areas dominated by public housing. If such influences are important they will be weakened progressively as the nature of the area changes with further sales and resales. Heath et al. also looked at council house purchasers as a specific sub-group. Their analysis suggested that council house purchasers were more likely to have voted Conservative than council tenants in general prior to purchase. Moreover, they found that purchasers were no more likely to defect to other parties than tenants as a whole (p. 49). Our sample is skewed both geographically and in terms of age. A more elderly group of southern oriented purchasers would be more likely Conservative voters than a younger, northern group. In previous research, for example, it was found that working class home owners in Consett were three times more likely to vote Conservative than council tenants in Cheltenham (Forrest and Murie, 1988a). In general terms the data in Table 2.4 would suggest that, in the period under consideration, among longstanding council house purchasers support for the Labour Party has not been dramatically eroded although there has been a significant drift towards the Conservatives and to a lesser degree to the Liberals, SLD and SDP. The survey provides no evidence either way that changed tenure status has been an important influence in shaping political loyalties.

Table 2.4
'Thinking about the past twenty years, which of these statements best describes how you voted in the last General Election?'

	London	Birmingham	All
Sample Number	110	134	244
	%	%	%
Always Conservative	13	31	22
Always Labour	39	40	40
Always Liberal	1	1	*
Used to support Conservative, now Labour	0	1	*
Used to support Conservative, now Liberals/SLD/SDP	0	1	*
Used to support Labour, now Conservative	14	10	11
Used to support Labour, now Liberals/SLD/SDP	4	2	3
Voted for several different parties	8	1	5
Did not vote	8	5	7
Don't know/No reply	14	7	10

* = Less than 1%

Because of rounding, figures may not total 100

Turning to health issues, it does appear that our samples are more likely than the average working class household to be covered by private medical insurance. Some 15 per cent of households in London and 6 per cent in Birmingham have access to private medical treatment. These figures are roughly comparable to general regional averages (OPCS, 1989) but are significantly higher than working class households as a whole. Private medical cover remains very much an attribute of white collar employment. In 1986, only 3 per cent of persons in the skilled manual category were either policy holders or covered by insurance policies (OPCS, 1989). This does not necessarily mean that we are dealing with a group of households with a particular set of values towards private provision. It would equally fit with the fact that this group are from particular job and income categories where private health provision is more common (perhaps through trade union negotiated agreements) than for skilled workers in general.

Both sets of households emerged as comfortably off and enthusiastic investors in privatized industries. Among the 244 households, 25 per cent owned stocks or shares. Of those, two-thirds of households had bought shares in recently privatized companies such as British Telecom or British Gas. Predictably, the London purchasers emerged as more affluent than their Birmingham counterparts, although not markedly so. For example, 58 per cent of the London group claimed to have neither (exceeding £3,000) savings nor investments compared to 65 per cent of Birmingham households.

Differences in the age profiles between the groups complicate their comparable wealth and income positions. Earned incomes are significantly higher among the London purchasers and the household income levels are boosted by the substantial number of households with multiple earners. Income profiles are also more polarized among the London households indicating a much greater contrast between earnings in work and income in retirement. Of those who provided details of household income (154), a quarter of London households but only 3 per cent of Birmingham had incomes in excess of £12,500 per annum. Given that this is a measure of *household* income few household members were in high earning occupations. In the low income categories (£5,000 p.a. or less) the figures were 21 per cent for London and 30 per cent for Birmingham.

Just over a third of all households claimed to have savings in excess of £3,000. On this measure there was little apparent difference between the two groups. Of those with savings over £3,000 (including stocks, shares, building society deposits, bank deposits), 25 per cent of households had more than £15,000. Ten households stated that they had assets of more than £25,000, excluding their house.

Given the apparent stability of their occupational histories it is surprising that a high proportion of households in both London and Birmingham contained a household member who had at some time received a redundancy payment - 31 per cent in both samples. Presumably, alternative employment was found immediately or they took early retirement. Savings had also been boosted by lump sums on retirement (22 per cent of households) and more than half the respondents (or their partners) were in occupational pension schemes. A small number (eight households) had received some form of inheritance. In two of those cases, the amount was in excess of £11,000.

Predictably, it is dwelling valuations which most clearly separates the two groups. Whereas only 2 per cent of London households own houses worth less than £50,000, virtually no-one in the Birmingham group values their dwelling above that figure. Moreover, whilst there is substantial overlap in Figure 2.1 there is some indication that prices have diverged further since purchase. This is complicated by the six year period over which the purchases occurred. And a higher proportion of London households bought in the latter half of that period (i.e. 1971-73). Given the rampant house price inflation at that time, a few years could make a considerable difference in property values. Nevertheless the point remains that two groups of households who at one time were paying very similar rents for similar use values are now occupying very different worlds as regards property exchange values and capital gains.

This also connects with claims that 'A family may gain more from the housing market in a few years than would be possible in savings from a lifetime of earnings' (Pahl, 1975, p. 291). The importance of occupational pensions and other savings and investments among the households in this study cautions against overstating the significance of housing wealth. Moreover, as has been pointed out elsewhere, much of the wealth in owner occupied housing is not easily realisable by the current generations of home owners. Leaving that aside, it is evident that few of the London households have savings approaching anything like the value of their dwellings. However, this is not quite so evident in Birmingham where an income stream from an occupational pension would fast overtake the money realized from the sale of a dwelling. And data about absolute gains from house price inflation demonstrate that in many areas the gains from the housing market are much lower. The relationship between housing wealth and other forms of savings and investments will vary both socially and spatially. Those tenants who purchased their dwellings in the late 1960s and early 'seventies came from a relatively privileged sector of the working class. Many of them were in secure, reasonably well paid, pensionable employment. For their material wellbeing in old age, the value of their pensions may be a more important factor than the value of their dwellings.

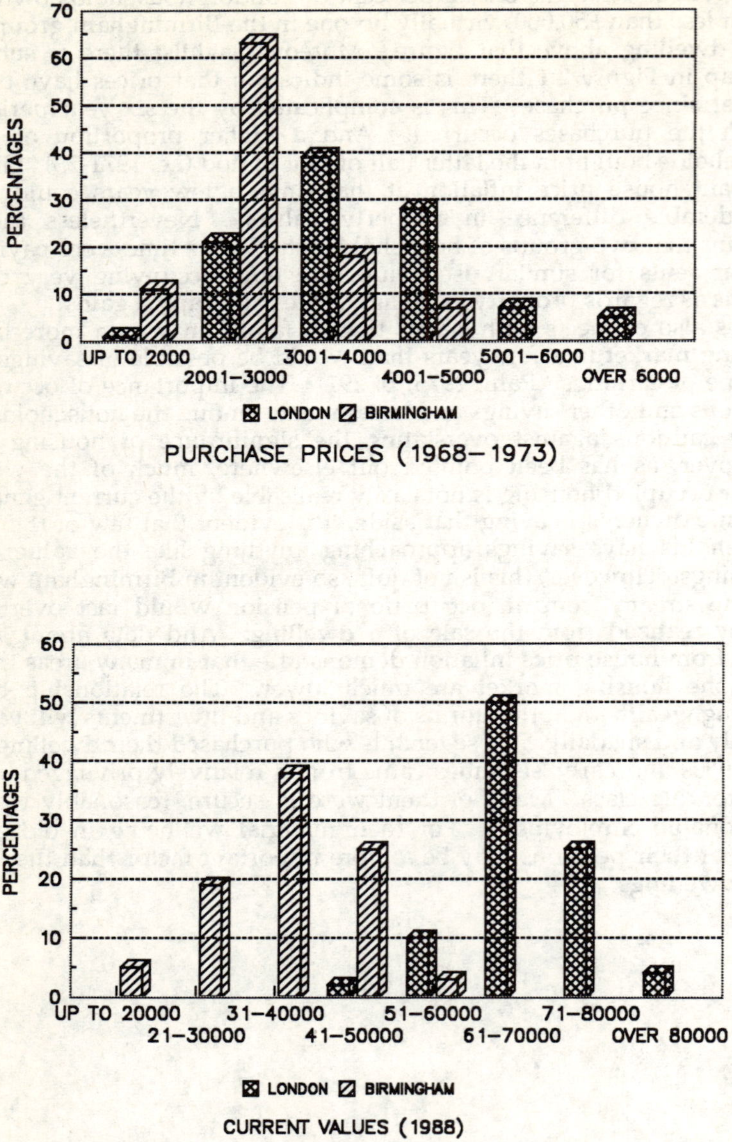

Figure 2.1 Purchase prices and current values of former council houses

Finally, what were general attitudes towards the council and council services? When asked to comment on the quality of council services in the area, there was a slightly muted measure of support. Comparable majorities in both London and Birmingham (57 per cent and 52 per cent respectively) agreed that services were good. Similarly comparable minorities (22 per cent and 23 per cent respectively) disagreed with the view that services were good. On a specific housing question the responses are rather more interesting. Whilst government policy has somewhat softened in tone in recent months, at the time of the survey there was considerable enthusiasm for transferring housing management functions to landlords other than local authorities. It might be expected that council house purchasers, more than council tenants, would support such a development. Indeed, given many of the impressions and claims in the literature regarding attitudes towards local councils by tenants, it is surprising that any measure of support exists for the local authority. More realistic responses are perhaps elicited when households are asked to choose between real alternatives. Too often, judgements are made about tenants' attitudes towards their local council from simple questions about dissatisfaction or satisfaction with existing services. Simply stated, they may be dissatisfied with state education in their area but it does not then follow that they believe the private sector would provide a better service. Similarly, it does not follow (as, for example, Saunders and Harris, 1988, suggest, p. 15) that council house purchase is an expression of dissatisfaction with council housing. For most households it has represented a sensible financial decision to buy a good quality dwelling at reasonable cost. Certainly, when asked to choose between the local authority and an alternative landlord to manage the remaining council properties in their areas, there is little indication of a general disillusionment with council management. An overwhelming majority, 75 per cent, would prefer to see the local authority remain as landlord. Whilst there is modest support for housing associations (12 per cent) there is virtually no-one in favour of building societies or private landlords.

Concluding Comments

The primary aim of this chapter has been to present new empirical information on what remains an extremely important area of social policy. At this level, the intention has been to provide a more rounded view of the impact of council house sales and to remind policy analysts and others that housing privatization has a much longer history than the election of the first Thatcher administration. By focusing on a group of tenants who bought their dwellings at least fifteen years ago we can begin to develop a longer term perspective on the social, political and economic impact of the sale of council houses. It has been stressed earlier that this group of tenants bought under very different conditions than those who have done so in the 1980s. Discounts were considerably smaller and for that reason, among others, the self-selected group who bought may be more exclusively among the more affluent council tenant households.

Moreover, rents were considerably lower in real terms, the economy was relatively buoyant, and council housing was an expanding form of housing provision. Indeed, the sale of council houses was a rather minor aspect of housing policy albeit associated with rather clearer ideological and political divisions than exist today. There is no suggestion therefore that the experiences of tenants buying today will mirror the experiences of those who bought during that period. On the contrary, it has been argued here and elsewhere that the impact of such a policy on households, on the social structure and on the wider economy is contingent upon a range of factors.

The chapter has engaged with a number of contemporary debates regarding the significance of tenure and tenure change and attitudes towards and experience of state provision of housing. Perhaps most importantly it has shown that so-called 'exiting' from the state sector can have very different forms and motivations. For the households in this survey the desire to buy could not be equated with a desire to leave the public sector in any simple sense. It is evident that their move into home ownership has in most cases been unproblematic and has enhanced their degree of satisfaction with their housing circumstances. However, the fact that in this case we are dealing with a group who have remained in the same dwellings underlines the significance of the public sector in providing the preconditions for successful and satisfactory home ownership. This runs counter to the views of those who interpret the mass sales which have occurred subsequently as undiluted expressions of dissatisfaction with public housing and public provision generally. This is not to deny the longstanding and deeply entrenched problems of old style paternalistic collectivism. However, the substantial sales of council dwellings which have occurred in the last twenty years combined with declining new public sector building have helped create a very different council housing sector from the one which existed when dwellings were bought by the tenants in this survey. These developments have set in motion a spiral of decline so that the experience of public housing may have become more oppressive, paternalistic and damaging for those households which remain. Their increasingly negative experiences are then used to explain mass exiting through sales. Such voluntaristic accounts of movements from the public sector to home ownership not only deny the very significant financial carrots and sticks involved but also the diversity of experiences of public housing.

It is also instructive to examine a group of sedentary households. The housing literature tends to be preoccupied with mobility and migration and to convey a sense of unrelenting household adjustment and movement. This is particularly true with the growth of home ownership with its dominant image of ladders and spiralling, socially aspirant, households. Highly mobile, long distance migrants are very much a minority of households. Most moves are very localized. There is an extensive literature on this aspect of housing market change which examines the social and spatial dimensions of residential mobility (see, for example, Murie et al., 1976). Implicit in much of this literature, however, is a view of non-mobility or limited mobility as an expression of constraint. And there is a developing argument that home owners adopt investment strategies in their housing histories which may necessitate a series of short distance moves to maximize capital gains and equity accumulation. This sample of households displays very different characteristics. As council tenants, many could have chosen to buy in the private sector and did not do so (Murie, 1975). Having bought, they did not use their purchase of a council house as a stepping stone to a dwelling which might have had more accumulative potential. From the responses in this survey, few have any intention of moving in the medium term. Non-movement has been a matter of choice - or has at least involved a range of non-financial constraints. The growing awareness of the significance of house price variations, capital gains and wealth transference associated with home ownership should not translate into the view that there is a mass tunnel vision developing whereby the 'house' and 'home' are evaluated simply in those terms. Of course a substantial number of the original purchasers have moved on and some may have done so for housing investment reasons. The point is simply to regain some balance in our assessment of people's orientations towards their housing.

In terms of occupational background, housing history, income, family structure and attitudes, the London and Birmingham households in this study emerge as very similar. The most notable contrast is in the value of their dwellings and the sums which may be passed on to their offspring. This is entirely predictable given relative rates of house price inflation in London and Birmingham. Debates about housing divisions within the working class tend to accentuate the developing gap between those who own and those who rent. But for those who were helped by state policy to enter home ownership through council house sales the potential rewards have been unevenly distributed. And the uneven pattern of house price inflation has been an important factor in this. In those terms, after fifteen or so years, the purchasers in London and Birmingham have moved further apart. Moreover, the full variation in the experience of council house purchase is not reflected in the data here. There are other areas with lower house prices than Birmingham and there are dwellings (e.g. non-traditional dwellings and flats) where rates of accumulation are lower.

However, for this sub-group of the original purchasers, the stronger message which comes across is of continuity and stability rather than dramatic change. It may be that the transformative effects of tenure change have been overstated, or at least overprivileged in accounts of the changing structure of British society. Part of the continuity can be found in the pattern and history of state intervention in working class housing provision. It was the relatively affluent, politically important, skilled labour aristocracy who gained most from the high quality council building programmes which followed the world wars. That same section of the working class have gained most from the sale of state dwellings. And it is this same group who have continued to gain (albeit differentially) from the promotion of home ownership in state policy. This succession of gains from state intervention in the housing market is not so easily achieved by those in weaker bargaining positions.

For council estates the implications of these data are also mainly about continuity and slow, cumulative change. Tenure conversion does not lead to a sudden change in the social composition of neighbourhoods. Ageing council tenants live alongside ageing home owners. If the latter groups are more inclined to move it is not a dramatic difference. Neighbourhood social change will occur slowly following owners' decisions to move on and this will generally be a long time after initial sale of dwellings.

3 The newcomers – who buys former council houses?

The research which has been carried out on council house sales has tended to concentrate on the characteristics of sitting tenant purchasers, the types of dwellings sold and the consequences of sales for remaining tenants and applicants. There is, however, another dimension to the sales policy which will become of increasing importance. This relates to what happens when former council houses are sold on the open market. A central issue for the reshaping of the housing market following significant privatization is 'where do former council dwellings fit into the market?' Do they form a new bottom end to the market with lower prices than other properties, so extending access to home ownership to groups otherwise unable to buy? And even if they perform this role, is access extended to the kinds of households who would have been allocated such houses had they become available for letting by the local authority? Or are former council houses, perhaps where their size and quality of construction makes them superior to much of the older private housing stock, more likely to be integrated somewhere into the middle of the market? In this event the only way in which lower income households or 'those who would have rented' would benefit, would be through a filtering process under which the prices of other properties would decline (or not rise as rapidly) because demand for them would fall with the increased supply of dwellings coming onto the market following council house sales.

In addition to these central questions - and related to them - are questions relating to whether the image of the former council house on a council estate reduces demand for such properties. Finally, in a period of rapid house price inflation and of considerable regional variation in house prices and housing demand it may be argued that the role of former council dwellings will vary considerably and reflect local and regional housing market circumstances.

There is very little existing evidence on these issues. Some evidence exists on rates of movement (Forrest and Murie, 1976) and there are the results from a postal survey of former council properties where the original purchaser was known to have moved (Forrest, 1980). This work was carried out in Birmingham. Previous work in Birmingham had shown that sitting tenant purchasers of council houses tended to be middle aged with a grown up family. The open market purchasers of these dwellings when they were resold were typically younger and at an earlier stage of the family cycle (Forrest, 1980).

> Typically, they have no family or one or two very young children. Social class differences are also apparent. As public sector dwellings become subject to allocation through market processes, the percentage of workers in white collar jobs rises from 19% to 36%. In parallel, the percentage in partly skilled employment falls from 25% to 11%. Whereas sitting tenant purchasers are a highly selected group of tenants in terms of income, age and position in the family cycle, the purchasers of former council houses are more directly comparable to first time buyers generally (Forrest, 1980).

This comparison between sitting tenant purchasers and open market purchasers also showed that about a quarter of the latter were previously owner occupiers, 57 per cent had previously been living with parents, 24 per cent had previously been tenants of a private landlord and only 8 per cent had moved from the public sector. The prices paid for former council houses did not indicate that they added an additional bottom rung to the housing market and purchasers could have bought elsewhere in the private sector - some had already done so. These impressions from a small study carried out in 1978 in Birmingham cannot be regarded as providing the last word on the issue. The belief that 'when a house is subsequently resold after the pre-exemption period, a cheap house for sale is provided which may well go to a family on the waiting list' (Rossi, 1977), still exists.

New Research Evidence

The research reported in this chapter provides new evidence from 1988 to develop discussion of these issues. Interviews were carried out at addresses in London and Birmingham. These were addresses of council houses sold to sitting tenants between 1968 and 1973. In London the samples were concentrated on two estates, Becontree and Harold Hill as previously described. In Birmingham a sample drawn from local authority records and used in a 1975 survey was used. Some 200 interviews were achieved in each city. Table 3.1 indicates that 43 per cent of those interviewed in London and 37 per cent in Birmingham were neither original purchasers nor their successors and had bought the property on the open market. From the household interviews it appeared that around half of these purchasers were the first open market purchasers - buying directly from the original sitting tenant purchasers. There were 42 per cent in London and 55 per cent in Birmingham for whom this was not the case.

Table 3.1
Nature of households interviewed in London and Birmingham

	London	Birmingham	Total
Sample Base:	197	219	423
	%	%	%
Sitting Tenant Purchaser still living at address	56	61	58
Successor	1	1	3
Open Market Purchaser/ Property had been resold	43	37	39

All the purchases in these samples were of houses. In Birmingham 72 per cent were three bedroomed houses, 23 per cent two bedroomed, and 2 per cent four bedroomed. In London the figures for these categories were respectively, 51 per cent, 41 per cent and 8 per cent. In London 46 per cent of respondents were male; in Birmingham, 51 per cent. Most of the properties had been bought by their current owner within the five years 1984-88 (67 per cent in London; 73 per cent in Birmingham). The prices paid depended on when they were bought, but one indication of market differences is that none of the Birmingham houses cost more than £50,000 and only one (1 per cent) cost over £40,000; in London, 19 per cent of houses cost over £50,000 and 34 per cent over £40,000. Only 8 per cent of purchasers in London and 9 per cent in Birmingham bought outright. Most of those buying with a mortgage obtained this from a building society (84 per cent in London, 89 per cent in Birmingham).

Social Class and Employment

Table 3.2 provides a profile of the economic status of open market purchasers at the time of interview. A small number of households had no earners, but most had one or two persons in paid employment. Few of the households included retired persons, and where they did, there was only one person in any paid employment. The vast majority of households consisted of one or more persons in employment and no-one in retirement. The social class distribution is skewed towards better paid occupations. White collar workers and non-manual workers were a significant group, and there were very few unskilled workers. As would be expected, this profile is much closer to that of the first-time buyer than of the new council tenant. Tables 3.3 and 3.4 add to this picture by providing some details on income and savings. The income data are heavily affected by refusals and a calculation which omits refusals is incorporated. It also refers to household income and while this is the relevant measure of income the accuracy of responses may vary where respondents do not know the incomes of other members of the household. There is no reason to believe this introduces any bias in the comparisons made. However, it may mean that income is underestimated and the figures can only be regarded as indicative and relevant for comparison within this study. Most incomes were over £7,500. One striking feature is that open market purchasers in London were substantially more likely to have incomes over £15,000. While refusals on this question mean that the results must be treated with caution, they are what would be expected given the prices paid for houses referred to earlier. The greater affluence of the London households is also indicated in Table 3.4. The most striking feature of this table, however, is the very high proportion of owners without significant savings or other assets.

Table 3.2
The occupational and economic status of Open Market Purchasers

	London	Birmingham
Sample No.	85	82
Respondent's work status	%	%
Full time work	59	60
Part time work	7	10
Housewife	26	21
Unemployed seeking work	1	2
Retired	5	9
Don't know/Other	2	2
Number of earners in household	%	%
Nil	9	15
1	42	37
2	42	45
3	5	4
4	-	-
5	1	-
Economic household type	%	%
Only 1 person in employment (full time) - None retired	41	34
More than 1 person in employment (full or part time) - None retired	38	50
Only 1 person in employment (full time) - at least one retired	1	1
No person in employment (or only 1 person part time) - None retired	5	7
No person in employment (or only 1 person part time) - At least one retired	4	7
Don't know	12	-
Social class	%	%
A	1	-
B	14	5
C1	18	24
C2	49	46
D	14	15
E	2	6
Don't know	1	4

Note: Because of rounding, figures may not total 100.

Table 3.3
Annual household income: Open Market Purchasers

	London		Birmingham	
Sample No.	85	(70*)	82	(48*)
	%	%	%	%
Up to £7,500	11	(13)	19	(33)
£7,501 - £15,000	31	(39)	28	(48)
Over £15,000	35	(43)	7	(13)
Don't know	5	(3)	4	(6)
Refused	18	(-)	41	(-)

* Omits refusals

Table 3.4
Non-housing savings and other assets of Open Market Purchasers

	London	Birmingham
Sample No.	85	82
	%	%
Bank or building society deposits over £3,000	25	11
Shares in recently privatized companies	14	10
Other stocks and shares	8	10
None	64	77

No households interviewed owned a second home or any dwelling other than the one they lived in. Households with bank or building society deposits of over £3,000 rarely had sums above £15,000.

Family Composition

Table 3.5 adds to the picture suggested by the economic profile of households. New purchasers tend to be in the early stages of their family and housing histories. The majority of respondents are under 35 and some three-quarters are under 45. However, this does not mean that young families with children are predominant. Young single persons and childless couples are well represented. Elderly and lone parent households - both groups strongly represented among new tenants - have very limited representation among open market purchasers. Where there are families with young children, there are rarely more than two children. Neither large families nor large adult households are common. No households consisted of more than six persons or had more than four children.

Table 3.5
Household and family composition: Open Market Purchasers

	London	Birmingham
Sample No.	85	82
Household size	%	%
1	9	17
2	39	35
3	19	21
4	26	18
5 or 6	7	8
Number of children under 16 in household	%	%
Nil	56	54
1	19	24
2	22	15
3 or 4	2	7
Household type	%	%
2 parents with 1 or 2 children	34	33
2 parents with more than 2 children	2	9
1 parent with 1 or 2 children	-	2
3 or more adults and 1 or more children	1	2
Young single person	7	11
Young childless couple	33	24
At least 3 adults and no children	6	2
2 adults (at least 1 elderly)	2	5
Single elderly person	1	4
Other	-	1
Don't know/refusal	13	6
Age of respondent	%	%
16-24	15	4
25-34	48	48
35-44	16	22
45-54	9	5
55-64	8	7
65 and over	3	6
Don't know/refusal	-	9

Table 3.5 (continued)

	London	Birmingham
Family composition at purchase	%	%
Single person	11	1
Childless couple	42	48
Couple with 1 child	24	11
Couple with 2 children	8	9
Couple with 3 or more children	4	7
Lone adult with 1 or more children	2	5
3 or more adults with 1 or more children	1	-
3 or more adults without children	7	-
Don't know	1	-
Household changes since purchase	%	%
Children born	22	29
Children left home	8	-
Parents/relatives moved in	-	4
Parents/relatives moved out	1	2
Divorced/separated	2	5
Remarried/partner moved in	4	2
Other	2	4
None	51	62
Don't know/Not applicable	14	-

A comparison between current household type and family composition at purchase confirms the view that households in a phase of family formation and growth are significant among purchasers. This was especially so in Birmingham, where 32 per cent of households already had children at the time of purchase, but 46 per cent had children at the time of interview. Comparable figures for the London sample were 39 per cent and 37 per cent. In the London households, children were more likely to have left home in this period. While the London and Birmingham groups are broadly similar, some differences in economic circumstances and family cycle stage are evident. Table 3.6 indicates other, albeit small, differences in relation to birthplace. In addition, interviewers coded 6 per cent of Birmingham and 1 per cent of London respondents as Afro-Caribbean or Asian. The lower priced Birmingham market appears to be open to a more heterogeneous group.

Table 3.7 provides details of housing history which develops this picture. The previous homes of the London sample were more likely to have been in the same neighbourhood or outside the city than the Birmingham sample. In addition, the London sample was more likely to have been living in a flat or maisonette, away from the parental home and to already have been an owner occupier. This previous tenure pattern applies to both respondent and partner. The cheaper properties in Birmingham are more likely to have been bought by first time buyers, those setting up a separate household for the first time and those in a phase of family growth.

Table 3.6
Birthplace of Open Market Purchasers

	London	Birmingham
Sample No.	85	82
Birthplace of respondent	%	%
Same city	75	60
Elsewhere in UK	20	27
Outside UK	4	11
Don't know/refusal	1	2

In the London estates where interviews were carried out, former council houses were more likely to be bought by more affluent households whose families were already established, and who were already owner occupiers. It remains the case that one in five purchasers in both cities were council tenants, that the properties bought had more bedrooms than those which were moved from, and that a significant proportion of those buying were moving to a house from some other form of accommodation.

Table 3.7
Housing history of Open Market Purchasers

	London	Birmingham
Sample No.	85	82
	%	%
Where living immediately before this house		
Same neighbourhood	42	27
Same city	34	57
Elsewhere	23	16
Previous dwelling type	%	%
House	56	77
Flat	28	17
Maisonette	12	2
Other	4	4
Previous dwelling size	%	%
1 bedroom/bedsit	9	13
2 bedrooms	31	24
3 bedrooms	51	52
4 bedrooms	8	7
5 or more bedrooms	1	2
Previous tenure	%	%
Owner occupier	47	30
Council tenant	21	20
Tenant of private landlord	6	9
Living with parents who were:		
owner occupiers	18	21
council tenants	5	10
tenants of private landlords	-	2
Living with friends/other relatives	2	4
Don't know	2	4
Partner's previous tenure	%	%
Owner occupier	48	26
Council tenant	19	21
Tenant of private landlord	5	6
Living with parents who were:		
owner occupiers	16	18
council tenants	8	16
tenants of private landlords	-	5
Living with friends/other relatives	4	4
Don't know	1	5

Choice of House

Respondents were asked a series of questions about their purchase of a former council house. As Table 3.8 shows, fewer than 10 per cent of purchasers did not know that the house had been a council property. Most of those who were aware thought this an advantage.

However, very few thought that the fact that the property was previously a council house was important. Their reasons for preferring the house related to a range of factors. While price was the most important of these, it was by no means the only one. It is relevant in this context that in 62 per cent of the households in London and 47 per cent in Birmingham, either the respondent or her/his partner had lived in a council property at some stage in the past and in 17 per cent and 20 per cent of cases respectively, one or other of them had been the tenant.

Table 3.8
Open Market Purchasers' attitude to former Council Houses

	London	Birmingham
Sample No	85	82
When you first became interested in buying this house did you know it had once been a council property?		
	%	%
Yes	93	90
No	7	9
When you finally decided to buy this house, why did you prefer it to any other properties available at the time?		
	%	%
Price	42	55
Location	16	27
Design/layout	14	24
Size	25	12
Condition/state of repair	8	6
Other	32	16
Don't know	4	-
When you finally decided to buy this house was the fact that it had once been a council property important to you?		
	%	%
Yes	8	1
No	92	98
Don't know	-	1

Discussion

The evidence presented above presents a clear picture of the purchasers of former council houses. They do not form a narrow category of new households, starters or first time buyers, nor do they represent a cross-section of households or buyers. They particularly include groups of younger households, without children, with growing families or with children leaving home. They are predominantly households with at least one person in paid employment and often with more than one. They include some affluent, multiple-earner households from white collar jobs with substantial other assets and trading up as home owners. Especially in London, many of the properties involved have not formed the point of first entry to home ownership, and do not form the bottom end of the home ownership market. From this evidence, the 'typical' open market purchaser is an affluent employed young household; a single person in her or his thirties or forties, or a married couple in the same age group starting or already having a family. Certain groups of households - the very young, the elderly, lone parents, the unemployed, are underrepresented. When compared with applicants or new tenants of council houses, these differences are significant and suggest a real redistribution of housing opportunities away from certain marginal groups. They also imply a real change in the social composition of council housing neighbourhoods.

It is appropriate to take this discussion of the relationship between reshaping the council sector and housing allocation policies further. Various studies show that there are concentrations of particular groups of households (in terms of ethnicity, gender, family structure, age, health status, bargaining power) in particular queues or entry routes into council housing. And different entry routes have different probabilities of allocation to particular parts of the stock. Subsequent mobility through transfers is significant in enabling initial allocations to be changed to fit preferences and needs. This feature of the operation of council housing has been widely experienced by council house purchasers whose history as council tenants has often included transfers to more desirable dwellings. In this situation any reduction in opportunities to transfer (especially from flats to houses) will have a disproportionate impact on those household types allocated to flats and maisonettes (in particular single parent families) and on households coming into council housing through those allocation routes which are most likely to lead to flats and maisonettes (homeless and waiting list). The opportunity to relax allocation constraints to enable a more varied pattern of allocation to particular household types and allocation categories will decline as sales and reduced new building affect the supply of houses to let. At the same time opportunities to modify these allocations through subsequent transfers will be affected. While all tenants and applicants will be affected by these changes, the most severe effects will be felt by those in the least desirable properties, those with least bargaining power and those where family structure or change imply a need for transfer.

The question of who would have been allocated to the dwellings referred to in this study had those dwellings still been council dwellings is a hypothetical one. Particular circumstances relating to time and place, queues, refusals and other elements of allocation policy and practice would affect the outcomes. Bearing this in mind, it is reasonable to make some general comparisons between the characteristics of open market purchasers and those of applicants for council housing and new council tenants. There is an appropriate source of data which reports a survey of new tenants and waiting list applicants in 25 local authorities in 1986 (Prescott-Clarke et al., 1988). While the direct comparisons presented in Table 3.9 may be affected by different practices in coding data, these are not likely to be significant. Other differences in survey method relating particularly to the member of household interviewed and the date of interview may be more important. For example, the economic activity status presented in Table 3.9 is affected by this. Nevertheless, the comparisons presented in Table 3.9 are striking. Open market purchasers are much more likely to be younger and especially to be in the 25-44 age band than applicants or new tenants. They are much less likely to be single person (elderly) or single parent households. They are much more likely to be in full time work. Almost 80 per cent of applicants and 86 per cent of new tenants had an income of less than £7,500 indicating much lower incomes than open market purchasers (Table 3.3). The low incomes and lack of savings of applicants on council waiting lists generally left them without a realistic opportunity of house purchase. New council tenants in this national study were much less likely to have been owner occupiers (18 per cent compared with 47 per cent of open market purchasers in London and 30 per cent in Birmingham). They were more likely to have been tenants or in lodgings (46 per cent) or living with friends or relatives (9 per cent). Comparisons with Table 3.7 also suggest that new tenants are equally likely to have moved to their new accommodation directly from the parental home. Where this was not the case they are likely to have been in less secure, lower standard accommodation.

Table 3.10 presents a similar comparison between new tenants and open market purchasers. This refers to the household type of new allocations in Birmingham in 1980/81 and the comparable data for open market purchasers. In comparison with existing tenants, new allocations involved a high proportion of lone parent households and single adult households. The latter are mainly elderly persons and would not be allocated to the types of dwelling in question here. To this extent the comparison is flawed. Nevertheless, large adult households are significantly underrepresented. Wider analysis of allocations in Birmingham shows that it is households being allocated through transfer and clearance routes which are most likely to be allocated to houses or bungalows. In this sense, it is important to recognize the impact of reducing choice and mobility within the council stock as well as initial access to it. An important aspect of mobility within the council housing stock relates to three bedroomed dwellings being released by 'declining households' moving to smaller dwellings (about one in five of all transfers in 1978/79 and 1980/81) and being used by growing households and those changing in the same bedroom category (40 per cent in 1978/79; 46 per cent in

1980/81). As the number of properties released by transfers to smaller dwellings declines as a result of council house sales, so the scope for this kind of movement is reduced - and the 'efficiency' of occupation of the stock as a whole will be affected. As opportunities to transfer decline, so the first allocation will become a permanent or longer-term allocation. Those whose first allocation is to a less satisfactory dwelling (and this relates to bargaining power and ability to wait) will be less likely to move to houses which, as their family circumstances change, they would choose to stay in and perhaps buy. The opportunities afforded by council housing to this generation of council tenants will, as a consequence, be very different from the opportunities of those who have purchased their council houses as a last stage in housing careers which, in the majority of cases, involved transfers between council dwellings.

Table 3.9
Applicants, Tenants and Open Market Purchasers compared

	Open Market Purchasers		Waiting[a] List Applicants	New[a] Council Tenants
	London	Birmingham		
	%	%	%	%
Age				
Under 25	15	4	23	36
25-34	48	48	15	20
35-44	16	22	8	9
45-54	9	5	9	6
55-64	8	7	14	9
65 and over	3	6	30	20
Don't know/refusal	-	9	-	-
Household type[b]				
1 adult only	11	21	48	40
2 or more adults, no children	49	48	32	21
1 adult and child(ren)	2	5	7	19
2 or more adults and child(ren)	37	27	12	19
Other/don't know	1	-	-	-
Economic activity status				
In full time work	59	60	39	29
In part time work	7	10	6	4
Unemployed seeking work	1	2	12	22
Retired	5	9	26	18
Other	28	23	17	26

a Prescott-Clarke, Allen and Morrissey, (1988)

b Moving group type. For open market purchasers and new tenants household type is at time of move.

Table 3.10
New allocations in Birmingham 1980/81
and Open Market Purchasers

	All	Transfers	New Tenants	Open Market Purchasers
Sample Base	351	115	236	82
	%	%	%	%
Single adult household	35	26	39	15
2 person adult household	18	13	20	29
1 parent and 1 or 2 children	12	10	13	2
2 parents and 1 or 2 children	20	24	17	33
1 parent and 3 or more children	2	4	2	-
2 parents and 3 or more children	5	8	3	9
3 or more adults with or without children	9	16	6	11

Source: Sample drawn from City of Birmingham, see Forrest and Murie, 1982.

The national data as well as those for Birmingham indicate that purchasers of former council houses have characteristics less like new tenants than those of original sitting tenant purchasers at the time that they bought. This is especially so in terms of employment and affluence. The clearest difference is that open market purchasers tend to be younger, are more likely to have smaller growing families and are more likely to be young, single persons or childless young couples. The older, large, adult households which formed an important group of sitting tenant purchasers are also evident among open market purchasers (see Murie, 1975, pp. 106-111). While this is likely to hold true in London as well as Birmingham the higher house prices associated with London sales appear to have resulted in a more affluent open market purchaser profile.

The conclusions drawn from this do not support the contention that redrawing the boundaries of the public and private housing markets has no impact on the longer term social role of the stock of dwellings built as council houses and subsequently privatized. When these houses are resold on the open market it cannot be assumed that they provide cheap houses for sale accessible to a family or any other household on the council waiting list. Privatization has moved the council stock out of reach of some applicants and potential new tenants. This is especially so in the higher priced London markets in this study. This spatial variation is a significant element which the previous limited evidence did not disclose. In other respects the data reported here are broadly comparable with those from ten years ago. Open market purchasers of former council houses are more comparable with first time buyers and are more affluent than new council tenants or applicants for council housing. Where the new data differ is in indicating that a substantial group of open market purchasers were previously owner occupiers (47 per cent in London). As such, and given their other characteristics, they are unlikely to have been on or contemplated being on the waiting list. Resold former council houses rarely benefit those on the waiting list and often do not even benefit first time buyers. The turnover of properties associated with moves to buy former council houses will generate supply elsewhere. How far this benefits some of those who would have rented remains unclear. However, it is clear that some of this turnover supply is of a lower standard - the former council house was preferred. It is also clear that for those households whose income, savings and other characteristics leave no opportunity to purchase, turnover supply to buy is not available and what is available to rent is often the less desirable parts of the stock. Just as council neighbourhoods with substantial sales will become more 'middle class' and less uniformly lower income and working class districts, so other neighbourhoods with few sales will become more ghettoized or residual one-class estates. The extent to which this occurs will vary from district to district depending on the size of the remaining stock and the social, economic and demographic structure of the district. This pattern of differential neighbourhood change, however, is likely to be common.

4 Moving on – propensities and strategies of tenant purchasers

There are now well over a million home owners who bought their properties as sitting tenants of local authorities or new towns. While there is considerable evidence about who buys (Murie, 1975; Foulis, 1985; Kerr, 1988) about reasons for buying and not buying (OPCS 1986; 1989) and about the wider impact and operation of council house sales policy, the subsequent behaviour of council house purchasers has not been researched. Evidence on the purchasers of former council properties has been presented in Chapter 3 but no evidence exists about the propensities of council house purchasers to move or not to move. At one level it may be assumed that such households will behave in the same way as other home owners with patterns of movement related to job, income and family cycle factors. However, there are reasons to doubt that this is the case. Council house purchasers are first time buyers but with a very different age, class and household type profile than the 'normal' first time buyer. They are also households who have moved tenure without moving house - whose achievement of home ownership has not involved the range of trade-offs and choices involved in most moves between and within tenures. They are also households who have expressed strong commitment to the dwelling rather than move to buy elsewhere. Finally, the terms under which they have bought are ones likely to affect mobility. High discounts and small mortgages relative to income provide real opportunities to trade up. At the same time restrictions on resale or (under the Right to Buy) loss of the advantages of discounts if resale occurs within specified periods (five years until legislative changes in 1988) provide a disincentive for movement in the early years following purchase.

In the light of these factors it is reasonable to suggest that council house purchasers will exhibit some special traits. At the opposite extremes it can be suggested that as an older group of first time buyers with a strong established commitment to their home, they are likely to be immobile and to behave much as they would have done if they had remained council tenants; or, that they will 'speculate' and move quickly once the related disincentives have run out or at key points such as retirement - in other words, their mobility will be greater than would have been the case if they had remained tenants. Previous evidence on rates of movement based on an analysis of electoral registers in Birmingham indicated that it is important to stress that this discussion is not about the loss of re-lets. If the pattern of movement for sitting tenant purchasers differs from that of tenants with similar characteristics, it is likely that this is at least partly because of tenure change. The loss of re-lets in council property relates to mobility if the properties had remained in council ownership and not to the actual behaviour of purchasers.

This chapter does not seek to resolve all of these issues but provides new evidence from the research carried out in 1988. In the first section it presents data based on return interviews carried out at addresses in Birmingham where a council house purchaser was previously interviewed in 1975. This enables some conclusions to be drawn about which households have moved on. The second section of the paper presents the results of a small number of interviews with original sitting tenant purchasers who have subsequently moved. Tracing and interviewing these households presents serious research problems which are discussed at various points (see Appendix). However, the resulting interviews are presented as illustrative cases which raise a range of questions about the opportunities created by initial purchase and the strategies pursued.

Movers and Non-Movers

The earliest study of council house purchasers was completed in Birmingham in 1975 (Murie, 1976). This included an analysis of the results of a sample survey. A sample of households which had bought their council houses in Birmingham between 1968 and 1973 was drawn from local authority records and 193 successful interviews were completed. The completed questionnaires were not destroyed and remain in the possession of the authors. In 1988 a new questionnaire was administered for all of the addresses in the original sample. The new questionnaire among other things sought to identify how many of the original purchasers were still living at the address concerned. Where the original purchaser was no longer present, the survey was designed to identify the characteristics of current occupiers. In the Birmingham sample as a whole, 134 of the 219 interviewed were the original sitting tenant purchasers.

Part of the research exercise involved attempting to trace movers and identify their housing experience since house purchase. However, because of the existence of the earlier survey data, it is possible to identify certain characteristics of movers without tracing them. Where an address is no longer occupied by the original purchaser, and an interview was completed with the original purchaser in 1975, it is possible to refer to that survey to identify various characteristics. For this purpose, a number of key variables from the 1973 survey were appended to 1988 interview schedules and included in computer analysis. This is a straightforward task. Of the 219 interviews completed in Birmingham in 1988, 146 were at the same address as a completed interview in 1973. Some details of the characteristics of the full 1973 sample are provided in Table 4.1.

An analysis of this group can be completed to look at the characteristics of original purchasers (from the 1973 survey) according to whether they are non-movers or movers (as shown in the 1988 survey). This is provided in Table 4.1. Of the 146 addresses, 97 were occupied at the time of the 1988 survey by the original sitting tenant purchaser; 49 had changed hands. Differences between non-movers and movers can be assessed in relation to a limited range of 1975 data relating to movement intentions, life cycle, economic circumstances, attitudes to the dwelling, purchase behaviour and tenure history.

Table 4.1
Characteristics of Sitting Tenant Purchasers according to whether they had moved over fifteen years later

	Original Sample	Non-movers	Movers
Sample No.	193	97	49
Whether intended to move	%	%	%
Yes	23	24	27
No	67	70	59
Don't know	9	6	14
Age of head of household at purchase		%	%
Under 35		6	18
35-45		26	22
46-54		46	37
55-64		·18	14
65 and over		3	8
No. of dependent children (in 1975)	%	%	%
None	47	51	43
1	18	18	16
2	16	11	24
3	8	8	10
4	7	8	4
5	4	4	2
No. of full time earners	%	%	%
None	5	2	6
1	47	45	45
2	35	40	31
3	10	9	14
4 or more	4	3	4
Social class of head of household	%	%	%
ii Intermediate occupations	10	9	8
iiia Skilled non-manual	9	7	16
iiib Skilled manual	45	42	45
iv Semi-skilled	31	33	20
v Unskilled	3	4	2
Retired	2	3	6
Don't know/refusal	1	1	21
Attitude to size of accommodation	%	%	%
Too small		13	14
About right		86	82
Too large		1	4

Table 4.1 (continued)

	Original Sample	Non-movers	Movers
Whether had improved home since purchase		%	%
Improvers		72	63
Non-improvers		28	37
Whether house nicer than others in area	%	%	%
Yes	64	63	69
No	24	25	18
Don't know	12	12	12
Whether satisfied with area	%	%	%
Yes	86	88	86
No	10	8	10
Don't know	4	4	4
Whether felt area had improved recently	%	%	%
Improved	13	16	6
Same	45	41	49
Deteriorated	40	40	43
Don't know	3	2	21
Feelings about purchase	%	%	%
Glad	93	88	98
Mixed feelings	6	10	-
Regret	1	2	-
Don't know	-	-	2
Mortgage amount	%	%	%
Bought outright	11	12	10
£1,000 or less	3	-	-
£1,001 - £2,000	13	18	6
£2,001 - £3,000	45	35	47
£3,001 or over	19	25	22
Don't know	8	9	10
Source of loan	%	%	%
Bought outright	11	12	10
Local authority loan	79	82	76
Loan from other financial institution	8	4	12
Don't know	2	1	2

Table 4.1 (continued)

	Original Sample	Non-movers	Movers
Mortgage repayment period	%	%	%
Up to 10 years	21	18	18
10-15 years	24	19	22
15-20 years	22	25	16
20-25 years	19	16	14
Over 25	12	6	18
Don't know	3	15	10
When first moved in to the dwelling		%	%
Pre 1953		35	12
1953-56		10	22
1957-60		7	6
1961-64		15	15
1965-68		22	27
1969-71		11	19
Previous tenure		%	%
Newly-formed household		4	8
Local authority		61	71
Private renting		20	10
Owner occupation		-	2
Don't know		14	8

(i) Movement intentions in 1975

In the 1975 survey, sitting tenant purchasers were asked about their plans for future moves. Actual non-movers (in 1988) were more likely to have had no intention of moving, and less likely to have been uncertain. To a limited extent then, original movement intentions varied between the two groups. However, the majority (59 per cent) of movers had not intended to move. Without evidence relating to reasons for moves (and about deaths, marital breakdown and other changes) it is not possible to evaluate this further.

(ii) Life cycle

The youngest and oldest heads of household and those with two or three children at time of purchase were most likely to have moved. Again, interpretation of these data is difficult especially in the absence of data on deaths. However, age characteristics at purchase were not such as to suggest a high rate of mortality and it seems likely that moves will have been associated either with retirement (the older households) or with demands for increased space (the younger households).

(iii) Economic circumstances

Mover households were less likely to be semi-skilled or unskilled workers, and more likely to be non-manual workers. However, distinctions in terms of social class are not dramatic. The number of earners in the household and the retirement status of households is compatible with the life cycle pattern outlined above. Movers were less likely to be in mid life cycle with two earners in the household and more likely to be either younger or more mature households.

(iv) Attitudes to the dwelling and area

In the original survey, sitting tenant purchasers were asked whether the dwelling was the right size for them, whether they had carried out improvements on the dwelling since they had bought it, whether they thought the dwelling was nicer than other council houses in the area, about their attitudes to the dwelling and area, and about their feelings about purchase. These factors could be taken as indications of satisfaction and as influences on movement. Movers do not display strikingly different attitudes on these variables. They are slightly less likely to have felt that their accommodation was about the right size, to have improved their house and to have felt that the area had improved. To this extent, they appear less satisfied with their dwelling. They are also slightly more likely to have considered their house nicer than others in the area and were more likely to express positive feelings about having purchased their house.

(v) Purchase behaviour

The council dwellings involved in this study are similar dwellings bought in the same period at similar prices. The data on house purchase show little difference between movers and non-movers in terms of purchase behaviour. Non-movers were slightly more likely to have bought outright or to have purchased with a local authority loan. The two groups show no significant differences in terms of deposit paid, the pattern of their approaches to other lending agencies and whether or not they had previously saved with a building society. Non-movers were more likely to have had over 25 years repayment period outstanding.

(vi) Tenure history and experience

Non-moving households were slightly less likely to have moved into the house they purchased as a newly formed household. They were more likely to have moved in from private renting and, most strikingly, to have moved in before 1955. The mover group were more likely to have moved to the house they bought more recently (in the last six years) and to have transferred within the council sector.

Moving Households

The data presented above do not describe two groups with dramatically different profiles. The non-movers are longer resident households and include more unskilled and semi-skilled manual workers. The mover group includes younger and older households and is a mixed category. Beyond this, it is best to conclude that the kinds of variables referred to above are not good predictors of mobility. Other factors associated with the housing, employment and family experience of households in the period since purchase would seem likely to explain movement - and these factors are not apparently strongly correlated with the variables referred to above. While the life cycle and economic factors indicated above operate in the way that would be expected, they do not have a lot of explanatory power and at least for a relatively homogeneous group such as the one referred to here, different kinds of complementary data are required. Nevertheless, on the basis of this evidence, it is clearly not possible to typify certain categories of households as likely to be carrying out a speculative purchase with plans to cash in on a speculative gain by moving. While such households may exist, they do not appear to be indicated either by stated movement intentions or household and economic characteristics.

In order to add to the picture presented above and to develop an appreciation of why sitting tenant purchasers move on, an attempt was made in this research to trace moving households. The interviews carried out both in Birmingham and London at the addresses of sold council homes identified properties where the original sitting tenant purchaser was no longer the occupier. In these cases the existing occupiers were asked if they knew where the original purchaser had gone. Following up these leads, referring to telephone directories and seeking to trace households through the Department of Social Security, enabled us to identify the present address of only a small number of moving households. It may be that those who had moved soonest and furthest and those whose property had changed hands more than once were most difficult to trace. The interviews carried out with council house purchasers who moved on cannot therefore be regarded as representative. The small number of completed interviews with these households do, however, present important illustrative examples. The interviews conducted with them mostly involved the administration of an extensive questionnaire with open-ended questions which provided the opportunity to record respondents' experience and attitudes in their words. Of the nine interviews which were completed in this way four were tape recorded and full use has been made of respondents' own comments in presenting the results of this stage of the research. In addition to this, telephone contact was made with seven original purchasers who had moved on. In these cases a full interview was not obtained but some limited information can be used. What follows then, is a presentation which refers briefly to seven cases and fully to nine other cases. Some of the latter interviews are used as case studies. In presenting and assessing all of these data and these cases in particular, it is relevant to bear in mind that while they may not be representative of the 'general' experience, they do represent real experience of individuals. It is not possible to indicate what proportion of all movers' experience would be broadly comparable with the range of experience presented here (and what proportion would be contrasting). Nor is it possible to indicate which cases are illustrative of the experience of a larger number of households and which of a smaller number. However, these limitations do not detract from the value of the data in presenting actual cases and experiences which are important in developing a perspective on the experience of home ownership.

Of the seven original purchasers identified through telephone interviews, six had bought in Birmingham and one in London. The information obtained shows that two of the dwellings sold had only been resold once (i.e. by the original purchaser); four had been resold twice; and one three times. In four of these cases it was possible to identify when the original purchaser moved (1973, 1974, 1976, 1986). In five cases it was possible to identify where the original purchaser had moved to. Three of these were local moves including one to Romford. The other two moves were from Birmingham to Water Orton just outside the city and to Brighton.

Of the full interviews being discussed in this section, six were completed with households which had bought homes as sitting council tenants in Birmingham, and three in London. It is this group that the remainder of this chapter focuses on. The initial discussion is in terms of the whole group. Key characteristics of the group derive from the way in which the interviews were generated. All of those interviewed bought council houses in the period 1968 to 1973 (Table 4.2). The house prices involved reflected the period. In Birmingham, purchase prices ranged from £2,500 to £2,900. In London the range was wider and the prices higher: £3,200, £4,875 and £8,000. All of the purchases were of two or three bedroomed houses. Three of the households were two person elderly retired households. These three households conform to the late family life cycle purchaser model. The chief wage earner was 48 or 49 years old at the time of the initial purchase. In each case the move had been associated with retirement, although in one case health status had also been important. The other six households would have been relatively young at the time of their first purchase (between 26 and 38). In this way the completed interviews do relate to the pattern indicated earlier. Those aged between 39 and 47 at the time of the initial purchase are not represented among traced interviews. The younger households interviewed were all two generation families. In two cases the youngest children were still in full time education. Four of these households had very young children when they first bought, but in all but one case, they had come to the end of family growth. In this one case two children had been born since the first house was purchased. The youngest child was fourteen in 1989.

The younger households interviewed had a wide range of reasons for moving. In two cases, reasons were connected with family size:

> Because I had got three adult children and I wanted a bigger place. (Interview 5)

> We wanted more room, more bedrooms; the rest of the house was all right but with the children we needed another bedroom. That was the only reason. (Interview 6)

Only one household referred to investment considerations:

> I was quite happy, but he talked about it - a lot were moving at that time and he worked it out that we could afford to move. A better investment we thought for the children. There's only so much you can do with an ex-council house. (Interview 9)

Other moves by younger households related to a divorce and 'wanting to make a fresh start' and to a desire to 'move to a better house or area'. (Interview 4)

> Well the environment, it was getting really rough. The council were allowing problem families to move in. We had a door smashed one night. It was just becoming a rough area. It had been a nice area when we first moved in but it gradually deteriorated, the older people dying and being replaced with problem families. We knew that we had got to move out, we must make the move or if it got any worse we wouldn't sell the house. (Interview 1)

> We always felt that was for a first time buyer and we always wanted a better house. (Interview 2)

The older households interviewed all made moves influenced by retirement. However, other factors were involved. In one case a reference to 'problem families' was similar to that mentioned above. The other considerations related to declining health status (arthritis) and to a changing property market which made it possible to sell a difficult to sell, steel-framed house and realize a preference to live in a 'better area'

(Interview 3). This household had bought a three bedroomed steel-framed house in 1970.

> The main thing was the property market had started to boom and it was the first real opportunity of getting rid of that type of property at a reasonable price. We'd retired and we wanted a better area in which to live.
>
> Our property was sold five times in one year. Consequently, we lost four houses prior to this one.

For another household, the reasons for selling related to family changes.

> I had got three adult children and I wanted a bigger place.

But the problems of selling were also important.

> We had been going for 18 months and we'd had numerous people down to look at the house but no one ever purchased it. Then out of the blue the local butcher came and bought it.... We liked this house and pressure to get a house - it took us 18 months to sell our other one. This was the only house available in the price range [that] we liked.

Table 4.2
House purchase experience of nine moving households

	Price of First Purchase	What Sold For	Price of Second Purchase	Estimate of Current Value	Other Aspects
	£	£	£	£	
1.	2,509	17,950	29,950	110,000	
2.	2,500	18,000	34,000	79,000	
3.	2,720	24,500	41,250	69,000	
4.	3,200	21,000	19,000	70,000	Mortgage payment difficulties connected with marital breakdown and health problems.
5.	2,900	16,000	24,750	60,000	
6.	2,850	11,350	12,100	55,000	Some limited leakage.
7.	2,500	19,000	20,000	40,000	Took out a new £1,000 mortgage to deal with repair problems in first house. Bought second house outright.
8.	8,000	80,000	68,000	100,000	Bought second house outright. Leakage paid for holiday, furnishings etc.
9.	4,875	45,500	72,500	81,000	Some limited leakage.

One of the households interviewed had lived for a period of six months (much longer than planned) in their mother's council house in between moving house. With this exception all had moved directly from their bought council house to their present house - and had moved only once. Only one household indicated an intention to move again. These are not highly mobile spiralists whose purchase of a council house has triggered active movement and investment strategies in housing. Nevertheless, all of them have made considerable financial gains from house purchase. Table 4.2 summarizes aspects of house purchase experience. This indicates that substantial gains were associated with the first purchase. However, after this there is greater variation. Two households traded down in price terms and two bought a house for little more than the price of the one they sold. Two of the older households purchased outright. The third took out a substantial mortgage (£19,000) but for a period of less than ten years. All of those borrowing in association with their second purchase borrowed from a building society, whereas all but one household had initially purchased with a local authority mortgage. Some households were able to use funds released when they moved house for other purposes. This leakage was most substantial for the household which traded down from the highest value dwelling. In contrast two households had experienced problems in relation to housing or finance. The most severe of these related to marital breakdown. In this context the employment and occupational characteristics of the household are important. Of the six younger households at the time of the interview, two had four persons in full time employment, two had three persons and two had two persons in full time employment. Only one household referred to a significant ($1\frac{1}{2}$ years) period of unemployment affecting the chief wage earner. All of these households had been married couples at the time of the original purchase. They were affluent, employed households usually with more than two incomes. In four cases a job change by the chief wage earner or partner was referred to as having been a promotion. None (including the retired reflecting on pre-retirement experience) referred to downward movement in employment terms. Five of the chief wage earners were in white collar managerial jobs - two with considerable supervisory tasks. Of the other households interviewed, two were (or had been) skilled workers and two semi-skilled or service sector workers.

The financial circumstances of these households differed more importantly in respect of income and savings. Household incomes varied considerably reflecting differences in occupation and in number of people in work. Respondents were asked about assets other than their home. Only two households had assets valued at over £8,000 or had more than one type of asset. Two households had no other assets, and four valued their total assets at below £3,000 (Table 4.3). The household with most assets had received two substantial lump sums (one for redundancy and one for retirement). Three of the others had received smaller lump sums of this type and one had inherited £3,000. Five of the six households not yet retired expected to benefit from a lump sum on retirement or on maturity of an insurance policy. All nine households were in an occupational pension scheme.

The general discussion of council housing and council house purchase places considerable emphasis on improvements made to properties and on attitudes to the tenure. These items are referred to in Tables 4.4 and 4.5.

Table 4.3
Ownership of assets other than the home they live in

	Household								
	1	2	3	4	5	6	7	8	9
Type of asset									
Another property									
Bank/Building Society deposits over £3,000	*	*	*	*				*	
Shares in recently privatized companies	*				*		*	*	
Other stocks or shares								*	
No other assets						*			*
Value of assets									
Under £3,000					*	*	*		*
£3,000 - £8,000		*	*	*					
£8,001 - £15,000	*								
£15,001 - £25,000									
£25,001 - £50,000								*	

Table 4.4
Major changes carried out to first property

	Household								
	1	2	3	4	5	6	7	8	9
New extension adding 1 or more rooms				*					*
Enlarged existing rooms through extension									*
Changed internal layout			*			*	*	*	
Refurbished kitchen	*		*				*	*	*
Refurbished bathroom/added shower in bathroom	*	*	*		*			*	*
Built garage									*
Built conservatory							*		
Built garden fencing	*			*	*		*		*
Installed central heating			*	*				*	
Installed new windows	*	*	*	*	*		*	*	*
Installed double glazing		*							
Replaced roof							*		*
Built porch		*		*	*			*	
Replaced wiring	*				*		*	*	*
Repointing carried out	*						*	*	*
Installed gas wall heaters					*				
Moved bathroom upstairs							*		

Table 4.4 indicates a substantial variation both in types and amount of improvement work carried out. The most common work involved replacement of windows and work to bathrooms. While purchasers were generally active investors in the fabric of their home, Table 4.4 suggests a high degree of satisfaction with their home prior to purchase. Dissatisfaction was highest with repairs and maintenance services and ability to move. Most striking however, are the high levels of satisfaction expressed about the council as a landlord, quality of accommodation, rent levels and security if circumstances changed. The greatest polarization of response existed over freedom to do what you wanted with your property and feeling it was your home. This range of responses relates to the discussion of tenure preferences in the next chapter. Attitudes to the council as landlord are not universally negative and decisions to buy are not reactions to negative views. For the small group of households being discussed, it is relevant to note one household very satisfied with six of the eight issues in Table 4.4. Furthermore, these high levels of satisfaction do not mean dissatisfaction with the current house. When asked about the comparison between their current and their previous (ex-council) home, the present home was preferred. Of the nine households involved, six felt their present home was better in terms of size; four in terms of quality of the building; nine in terms of design/layout; seven in terms of investment; two in terms of proximity to relatives or friends; seven in terms of environment; and seven in terms of safety. Where households did not think their present home was better, they generally regarded it as the same. Only in terms of proximity to shops and amenities (four households) and public transport (two) did more than one household feel their present home was worse. Consistent with these data the nine households involved generally said they were very satisfied or fairly satisfied with the items referred to in Table 4.5 (excluding the first) in relation to home ownership. One household was very dissatisfied with ability to move. With this exception none expressed any dissatisfaction. Three households stated that they were neither satisfied nor dissatisfied with home ownership in terms of security if circumstances changed.

The final general issue covered by these interviews related to use of public services and voting behaviour. In Chapter 2 of this book it was suggested that the early purchasers of council houses had not adopted new political attitudes and privatized consumption practices. The nine moving households interviewed are similar. Only one was covered by a private health insurance. None disagreed that the quality of council services was good overall. Most of the households made some use of public services: all used a family practitioner; six used public transport; six used public libraries; two had children at state schools; and one used adult education facilities. Voting behaviour also indicated considerable continuity, but some change towards the Conservative party. Of eight responding, two had always voted Conservative and two had always voted Labour. Two households said they used to vote Labour but had changed to Conservative.

Table 4.5
Satisfaction with council housing

	Very satisfied	Fairly satisfied	Neither satisfied nor dissatisfied	Very dissatisfied	Fairly dissatisfied	No opinion
General feeling about the council as a landlord	2	6	1	-	-	-
Quality of the accommodation	2	4	1	2	-	-
Feeling repairs and maintenance done	1	1	2	3	2	-
Feeling it was your own home	4	1	-	4	-	-
Rent levels	3	4	2	-	-	-
Ability to move or get a transfer	1	2	1	1	3	1
Freedom to do what you wanted with your property	1	4	-	2	1	1
Security if your circumstances change	1	5	1	1	-	1

Illustrative Cases

The general picture outlined above can be developed more fully through individual case studies. In this final section of this chapter four case studies are referred to in order to highlight the different experience of mobility and housing. These cases are presented in a summary form with some longer verbatim quotes where these illustrate particular themes. The principal emphasis in these cases is on reasons for moving. They are particularly of interest in the context of debates about household moving strategies.

The skilled worker

Mr and Mrs Key bought their council house in Kings Heath, Birmingham in May 1968. The house was a post-war, two bedroomed terraced house in a block of four built on a bend in the road. As the end terraced house it had plenty of land at the side and a large garden. The house did not have central heating, but the Keys felt it was about the right size. At the time, Mr Key was 32 and working full time as a semi-skilled machinist in the motor industry. Mrs Key was 28 and working part time. There were two sons in the family, aged five and two. The Keys had previously been Birmingham tenants and had moved to their home through a transfer. The Keys had first found out that they could buy from friends. They had not considered buying another house:

> We were paying a decent rent and as rents were going up, we thought we would be better to buy. As it turned out, the mortgage was only 50p more. (Interview, 1975)

The Keys bought the house (with a discount) for £2,850 and paid a £25 deposit. They borrowed from the council and did not approach any other lender. They had never saved with a building society. At the time of the 1974 interview, the Keys had not made any improvements to the house other than installing a new coloured bathroom suite. They estimated that they had spent about £15 each year on maintenance and repairs. This was less than anticipated but paying for repairs was identified as a disadvantage of ownership. The Keys regarded the house as nicer than most council houses in the district

> .... it's more modern and we have a nice big garden.

Although their immediate neighbours had not bought, most of their friends were glad to have bought

> ....it's security - plus the way rents are going up, we'd be paying and paying with nothing to show for it - I would have felt out of it with all my friends being owner occupiers. Always the possibility of buying a better and bigger place - always the security.... getting better response if you say you are buying your house.

At this stage, the Keys did not think they would move from the house. Their mortgage repayments were £22 per month compared with the previous rent of £19 per month. They estimated the value of the house at £8,000 (an increase of 186 per cent). They identified clear advantages of renting:

> All repairs are done for you - plus if you do want to move you can get a transfer without the worry of buying or selling

and disadvantages:

> The rents can go on and on, its dead money, and the repairs aren't always done when you want them. You can't choose the neighbourhood.

The Keys remained in the Kings Heath house until 1978. During that period, a third child, a daughter, was born. They changed the internal layout of the house but compared with other households, remained inactive improvers. They sold the house for £11,350 and moved a very short distance within Kings Heath. The main reason for moving was to obtain more room (interview 6, above). In addition to the number of bedrooms, the house they moved to had larger bedrooms than in a lot of the houses they looked at. They also referred to

> .... size of the kitchen (and) the district. We didn't want to move out of the district and the price was right - we couldn't afford a big mortgage.

The new house cost £12,100 - only slightly more than the house they sold. However, their building society mortgage was considerably larger than previously (£6,000), leaving £2,425 which

> .... paid the solicitor, had new carpets, new furniture, and a couple of thousand in the bank - some of that was for the central heating.

At the time of interview in 1989, the Keys estimated the value of their house at £55,000. They did not have any other assets. Mr Key had remained in employment throughout and continued to work as a skilled craftsman in car components manufacturing. His job involved participation in an occupational pension scheme, but otherwise he had expectations only of a small (£2,000) lump sum from an insurance policy. He thought that 'having something to pass on to a relative' was a 'not very important' feature of home ownership. With their daughter still at school, one son qualified and working as a chef, a second son on a government training scheme and Mrs Key in part time low paid work the Keys remained heavy users of public services and their combined household income was below £15,000. Their general situation does not appear to have been transformed by home ownership.

The affluent home owner

Mr and Mrs Black bought their council house in Billesley, Birmingham, in March 1968. The house was an inter-war three bedroomed, end-of-terrace house with ample space at the side. It did not have central heating and had an outside toilet only but was felt to be about the right size. When they bought their home Mr Black was 30 and working full time in light engineering in a skilled job. Mrs Black was 22 and not working. Their two children were aged five and two. They had moved to their present house from a previous council owned house. The Blacks had first found out that they could buy their house from the information in a local authority circular. They had not considered buying any other house. They bought the house for £2,509 benefiting from a small discount, paying a £5 deposit, and obtaining a local authority loan. Their 1974 estimate of value was £7,500. They did not approach any other lender and had never saved with a building society. At £21.75 per month their mortgage was low enough to have influenced the decision to buy

> .... basically because the rents were going up and it didn't work out much different between buying and renting.

At the time of the 1974 interview, the Blacks had three children, with a son aged four. They had spent a considerable amount of money on the property. They had moved the toilet inside, altered the kitchen and installed a new bathroom suite and kitchen units. Because of this their estimate of annual expenditure on maintenance and repairs was £500 - about what they had expected. The Blacks did not think their house was better than others in the district and although they thought the area had deteriorated in the last few years, were satisfied with it. Their immediate neighbours had not bought their home but most of their friends were owner occupiers. They said that they were glad they had bought

> The way the rents are going up, our mortgage payments are much the same as the rent was. You are getting the house in the end.

In 1974, the Blacks thought that they would move within the next ten years,

> I'd like a new house. It would be a newer property; same size still, though. Wouldn't buy where there were so many council houses.

Prior to buying, the Blacks were paying £4.50 per week in rent. They referred to the advantages of renting as

> .... repairs are done .... if you want to move it is easier

and disadvantages

> .... you can't do what you like to the house - you have to have permission for everything.

The Blacks remained in Billesley until 1980 when they sold the house for £17,950. In the period since 1974, they had continued to carry out improvements. In their 1989 interview they referred to new garden fencing, new windows, replaced wiring and repointing as well as to a refurbished kitchen and bathroom. They moved out within the same segment of the city to Hall Green - to a house with the same number of bedrooms. Their reasons for moving were associated with the changing nature of the area (interview 1 above). The area they moved to

> .... had got a good reputation and my wife wanted a brand new house. We knew in this area there were no council houses, everybody were owner occupiers and looked after their houses.

Their new house was, at £29,950, significantly more expensive than the one they sold. They took out a much larger (£13,000) endowment mortgage and put all the proceeds from the sale of the previous house into the new home. This greater financial commitment was made easier by Mr Black's 'promotion to a manager' and by the earnings of other members of the household. By 1989 their three children had completed full time education. One had left home but the other two were living at home and in full time employment. Mr and Mrs Black and one daughter (in banking) were in well paid managerial jobs. Mrs Black was branch manageress of a dry cleaners and Mr Black a stock control manager in engineering. As well as having the highest household income of the households interviewed, the Blacks would receive a substantial lump sum associated with an insurance policy. They had substantial savings including shares in recently privatized companies. Their general situation in 1989 was significantly different from 1968 and 1974 but as well as family cycle changes, promotion and increased incomes are significant.

The mobile home owners

Mr and Mrs Carr bought their three bedroomed council house in Lyndcroft Road, Birmingham in 1973. They paid £2,500 for it and bought with a fifteen year local authority mortgage. They were not included in the original 1974 survey and it is the 1989 survey data which illustrate a different experience of mobility. In 1989 Mr Carr was 65 and had retired from his job as a skilled telecommunications engineer. Mrs Carr was 57 and working part time as an auxiliary district nurse. Their six children had all left home although only one was living outside the West Midlands. The Carrs illustrate a different experience of home ownership. Following their original purchase, they experienced problems with repairs and repair costs and 'needed an additional mortgage of £1,000 for modernization to bring it up to standard'. They were active improvers and during their stay at the original house moved the bathroom upstairs, refurbished the kitchen, changed the internal layout of the house, added a conservatory and had substantial work carried out on garden fencing, new windows, replacing the roof, rewiring and repointing. When they sold the house for £19,000, their progress through home ownership appears to have been similar to the Keys and the Blacks. Their main reason for moving was:

> .... to improve our future environment and accommodation prior to retirement really - the area was slowly being taken over by some undesirables, deteriorating, problem families in council houses doing nothing to help themselves and for all your efforts to improve your property it was counteracted by their lethargy.

In choosing a new home:

> .... we were impressed with the modern mobile homes and this one became available at the right price, and in an area which we liked. A mobile home was within the money that we could get for our house, was the nearest thing to a brick bungalow in a country area that fell into our finances - what we were going to get for (previous house).

They bought a mobile home on the edge of Birmingham, in Worcestershire, for £20,000. The money released by the sale of their previous house 'just bought it - this cost a little bit more, used £1,000 from my savings'.

Mr Carr had received a lump sum of £10,000 on retirement. By 1989 the Carrs stated that they had under £3,000 in all savings and assets other than their home (valued at £40,000) and including shares in recently privatized companies. The long history of skilled work in the same kind of job but unbroken by unemployment was similar to the Keys. It had not left them with substantial assets or room to manoeuvre in housing or other spheres. However, it is the Carr's own unprompted summing-up of their experience that is most striking.

> Me and my wife are part of many ex-council and private who have invested any monetary benefits in providing themselves with a safe and environmentally pleasant home - a mobility type park home - for the future, their retirement, so relieving the burden of the local council to provide accommodation. The point is many of us now feel we have gone back into the clutches of unscrupulous land owners. The Mobile House Act of 1983 is open to abuse by the landlords, who can give a feeling of insecurity to the residents of these mobile park homes. Also rent increases - that is, ground rent - it's uncontrolled, you're in their mercy - everything you own in your life is on their little plot of ground. Unlike most people under the law who can buy the freehold, this is denied to park house people. We are very, very happy here but we don't like to have the uncertainty of the unknown as we don't actually own the ground.

Moving to the seaside

Mr and Mrs Locke were aged 69 and 68 respectively in 1989. They had bought their council house in Wincanton Road, Harold Hill in 1968 for £8,600. This was after a discount 'It was something like 15 per cent or something. It sounded very reasonable, anyway'. Mr Locke obtained a mortgage from Prudential Assurance.

> The reason I picked the Prudential was because I had quite a large life assurance - life insurance - with them, and because of that they tied one into the other because in those days it wasn't so easy to get mortgages as they would let you think nowadays....
>
> Well, in those days it wasn't easy. You know, people wouldn't lend you money unless you had some collateral, and we didn't have very much collateral. I know we had to borrow £5,500....
>
> £5,500 I borrowed on a 17 year mortgage, with my life insurance as collateral.
>
> There were no problems with the mortgage, that just ran on. I had it on a fixed nine and a half per cent which seems slightly higher than what you could have got at the start off ....

When asked about any improvements made, Mr Locke stated

> I had a very elaborate shed, if you might call it, added onto the garage, which meant instead of keeping the lawn mower and things in the garage I kept them.... I had two rooms knocked into one by knocking down the dividing wall, which made a very big room.... we made our lounge twice the size. We did have kitchen units put in at some stage. We had the bathroom tiles and a better suite put in instead of the old council type.

Mr Locke also renewed the garden fencing, installed new windows and central heating, built a porch and had rewiring and repointing carried out. The house was sold for £80,000. Mr Locke offered a number of observations on the comparison between his current and former house:

> The former was about three times the size. It was a lot bigger.... you wouldn't get much better than those council houses that were built.... That was a fantastic housing estate that they built just after the war. Money was obviously no object, it was built to a standard of building that they'd never do again, when labour wasn't a problem. For instance, I don't know whether its technical enough for you, all the inside bricks of the house were brick. You'd never do that now. All the inside walls are concrete and breeze blocks and stuff. They were double brick, beautifully built. Every repair, when I had the windows taken out, they said 'You'd never get houses built like this any more'. But the reason was that they were built in the 1946 period, 1947-1948. They used German and Italian prisoners of war, time wasn't a problem, labour wasn't a problem and they were built beautifully. You won't get houses built to that state, and eight to an acre. Now they build 'em twenty-four to an acre.
>
> [The present house] couldn't be better. It couldn't be better than that one, so it must be worse - this is good quality built by a builder, but they were superlative ....
>
> This is better for us now, because our circumstances have changed. The other suited us when we had a family and parents living with us, then that was - we needed a big four bedroomed house. It was really a five bedroomed house. We don't need it, so we had a two bedroom....
>
> The other one is already worth about £150,000. But it suited us. We wanted to get away to the seaside and to retire and so money wasn't the important part of that. But that house would be a much better buy for the people who bought it....

When asked about his view of the council as a landlord Mr Locke stated:

> I was very satisfied with them, I thought they did a good job.
>
> Getting repairs and maintenance done was not very easy, but we must remember too, that the house I sold wasn't the ordinary council house, it was a leasehold, you had to sign a lease for it. It was a higher income sort of house you see.

It was a higher income group house, and you had to sign when you first went in there, although this did change. When you had them you had to sign a lease for seven years and you had to pay monthly and you had to give satisfactory notes and things like that, although in later years of Ken Livingstone, ILEA and that sort of thing, all was washed aside and they became units of accommodation and most of the people who lived in those houses then moved out because being big houses they moved in problem families who tend to have big families you see, and it was a bit unfortunate, they did tend to... lovely big four or five bedroomed houses, they didn't put them on a lease again to doctors, solicitors, teachers - who were there when I went - who could afford the higher rents. But then, when they became units of accommodation they moved in with between seven and eight children. It changed.

When asked the main reason for deciding to move from the initial home Mr Locke said

The main reason was I think, because my wife has arthritis and she can't walk up and down hills and we were on a hill.... and we wanted something flat, and down on the sea shore we can walk to the houses, walk to the buses (if we ever need to), walk to the sea shore, if unfortunately I wasn't able to be here, and so it was for domestic comfort.

The main reason for choosing this particular home was that

.... my wife liked it best of all the ones we saw. You get these dreams of retiring to Sussex, retiring to the sea, it had to be near the sea. We both wanted to be able to walk along the sea shore and this Sussex coast seemed the most climatically suitable; Essex is too windy, Margate is too breezy, and it is easy to get up to London, we are still Londoners and we still go up there, we could get there faster than I used to be able to from Essex. It seems strange, an hour and a quarter to Victoria. Great, if I had known what I know now I would have moved down years ago and commuted.

The Lockes bought their new house outright for £68,000.

Well, I have probably spent £10,000 on it; I would think it would probably be worth about £100,000.

There was only a few thousand left. We didn't lose anything out of it, in fact I gained a couple of thousand pounds. We used it by going down the Nile on a holiday and we cruised down to Luxor, so we spent £4,000 on that, and that evened us all up.

I spent a lot of money. I had a new lounge put on, I will show you, that was an electric fire and that cost a lot of money. It is a wood fire now, we have logs burning, which I always wanted. I didn't want central heating. For looking at, for pretty decoration. I spent quite a few thousand on little bits and pieces. Curtains, carpets, with which you can lose two thousand so quickly.

The Lockes had no plans to move. Mr Locke had bought his home when he was 48. For the next fourteen years until his retirement, he worked for the same company.

> I worked for the same company for 36 years, but of course, I was fortunate, I got on and did well. You don't know that when you start off.

Mr Locke had been promoted and was not unemployed at any stage. By the time he retired he was export controller, a divisional manager of an international company. Mrs Locke had a part time job, as a hospital librarian. It started off being voluntary and later became paid employment.

Asked about savings, Mr Locke referred to deposits of over £3,000; shares in privatized companies and other stocks and shares. Mr Locke had received both a lump sum of £16,000 on retirement, and a redundancy payment of £17,000.

> Yes, I got a redundancy payment. That was a fiddle really. The company called me redundant, as I retired at 62 and not 65.

Conclusions

What do these illustrative cases suggest? The Keys are a working class family whose physical housing situation has not been significantly changed through house purchase. They moved locally to a larger house in the same price range. With their larger family they would have qualified for such a house through a transfer. In this way it is unlikely that becoming a home owner has changed their physical housing conditions. The Keys were not active improvers and had not expressed their ownership through investment in refurbishing either of their houses. Similarly there is no indication that the Keys' lifestyle had been transformed in other ways. Their room to manoeuvre was affected by a young and growing family and relatively low income, rather than by home ownership status. In these terms the Keys' immediate situation has only been altered in one respect. They are owners of an appreciating asset. This has not resulted in an improvement of housing or other consumption and has not transformed their income, family or class position. What then does ownership mean? It could be argued that the benefits of ownership are future benefits. Either they relate to a rescheduling of housing costs or to benefits accruing to the next generation. Different issues are relevant here. House purchase would mean that at some stage, (after another fourteen years in the Keys' case) regular monthly payment would end. However, repair and maintenance costs could increase. There is a rescheduling of housing costs over the lifetime, but it is not clear what the exact nature of rescheduling is. On the other hand, it is argued that the real effects of house purchase are only realized through inheritance. In this context it is relevant to note that there are three children to inherit and that, depending on their work careers, the level of inheritance cannot be regarded as sufficient to generate access to housing superior to that achieved by their parents as tenants.

In most ways the Keys' situation has not changed. They have, however, become owners and wealth holders. What that means in social and economic terms relates to discussions about the ability to realize wealth. Realization is not likely except through the next generation. It is possible to argue (as Saunders does) that home ownership is qualitatively different from ownership of other saleable assets and that it represents a different sense of security. Equally, it may be argued that moving into the market merely involves a change in management and ownership regimes reflecting institutional, economic and political demands rather than individual demand or increased consumer satisfaction. It makes no difference to the owner but does to others.

The Carrs' situation raises these questions even more starkly, because in one important respect their housing situation had become less secure and controllable. The asset value of their mobile home was much lower. In this case six children would be beneficiaries of a much smaller estate. In the Carrs' case, their mobile home is home ownership. But the insecurity and lack of control over key elements including ground rent does not lead them to emphasise the qualitatively different sense of belonging. In this context it is accumulation which could be seen to represent the key difference between their actual situation and the situation they would have been in had they not bought. The value of their property is relatively low. More importantly, it will not necessarily continue to grow and could decline. This partly reflects the nature of the property, demand for it, processes of obsolescence and management. In this context it is possible that the Carrs' experience will be of declining housing quality and security with limited market capacity to remedy the situation by moving elsewhere. What is more, the capacity for realization of wealth is not only restricted to the next generation but is too small to have a major impact on that generation's life chances. This situation reflects housing decisions. However its context is that of a stable work history without the progression or promotion experienced by the Blacks or the Lockes.

The Carrs' history contains another element also illustrated by the Blacks. In both cases the households were satisfied with their council housing - sufficiently so to buy the house. In neither case did individual ownership prevent concern about neighbourhood change developing. In this sense the desire for home ownership was not sufficient to lead them to move house; but nor was the status of home ownership sufficient to prevent dissatisfaction with the neighbourhood from arising. The lesson would appear to be that explanations for decisions do not rest solely or even primarily on ownership issues.

The Blacks were at a slightly later stage in the family life cycle than the Keys. However, the more important distinction in their experience relates to employment history. Greater affluence enabled more active investment in improving properties and in trading up. It also enabled them to accumulate savings and buy stocks and shares. To this extent their experience of asset holding is wider than of housing alone and reflects an income and employment situation and stage in the family cycle which differs significantly from the Keys'.

Finally, the Lockes' position has many of the elements of the Blacks' especially in relation to job career and promotion. In addition it highlights issues about the different experience of council housing. Rather than living in a difficult to sell, steel-framed house, they had lived in a very high quality, well built house. The Lockes regarded this house as better in size, in quality of building and as an investment than the house they subsequently moved to. They also were very positive in their attitudes to the council as a landlord. Nor was their subsequent sale of this property particularly affected by negative feelings. Health circumstances and dreams of retiring to Sussex were the dominant considerations. In terms of wealth and accumulation, the Lockes felt that by moving they had probably reduced their rate of accumulation. Their housing moves were neither investment led nor investment maximising. They were led by concern to obtain the best housing for their current circumstances and the greatest satisfaction in use. Crucial to their situation, as with the Blacks, was employment and financial security. In retirement it is this rather than housing related differences which is the crucial aspect of social differentiation.

Research which focuses on housing and housing tenure can too easily fall into the trap that it is housing decisions and changes which explain other changes. Thus, there is a tendency to look at the changing circumstances of households who have bought their council houses and account for any other changes in their situation as emanating from changed tenure status. In the histories and descriptions presented above housing changes have been strongly emphasized. This need not mean that they are seen to be the most important factor in family histories. Life cycle changes and employment histories have also been referred to. The households referred to above have very similar origins in housing terms. They form a selected, privileged group who were tenants of properties (generally with similar values) which they and they alone could buy. From these similar origins the households have arrived at various housing destinations. In assessing this, key issues arise. Firstly, are the various destinations all that different? All are still home owners and although their properties vary from a relatively low value, less than wholly secure, mobile home to properties valued at over £100,000, they remain a relatively narrow sector of the housing market. Secondly it would appear that differences in income, savings, and investments are greater than differences in housing. Rather than housing being the key to social difference or home ownership summing up the circumstances, opportunities and life chances of this group, differences associated particularly with income and employment offer a stronger indication of command over resources. Thus, the estimated value of properties tends to be lowest amongst those who were in unskilled and semi-skilled jobs. Leaving aside the retired there is a consistent relationship between job, income, other assets and property value. The differences within this group are related to their work and are not upset or cut across by housing factors. In order to understand what is happening to these households, it is important to start with an account of their employment, work careers, and household incomes. Differences associated with housing make most sense in the light of this. This is not to say that in comparing this group with other groups - perhaps those who had not bought as sitting tenants - housing situation would be unimportant. Indeed it might be more important especially when compared with the situation of buyers on the private market or with subsequent council house purchasers buying with larger discounts. In such comparisons, the terms and circumstances around purchase are likely to enable some lower income households to leapfrog higher income groups. However, this dislocation is likely to be modified, as continuing income differences reassert themselves in determining command over resources.

This perspective comes back to the discussion of the importance of housing wealth and its use and how far it can be realized. Among the group described here, leakage has been limited but greatest among those with highest incomes. This is partly because lower income and older households will prefer to minimize borrowing and so will reinvest the proceeds of a previous sale. In terms of the benefits to the next generation, it has been argued that these will also tend to vary in a manner consistent with job and income.

One issue which has not been discussed is the rate of return on investment. Some accounts of rate of return refer to an arithmetical calculation of the ratio of deposit to increased value (Saunders and Harris, 1988). This is an unsatisfactory basis for calculation (Forrest et al., 1990; Murie, 1990). The illustrative cases above demonstrate one way in which it is unsatisfactory. Households making a massive rate of return initially, cut their rate of return dramatically by moving and by increasing their deposit through reinvesting the proceeds of the previous sale. The assessment of the advantages of purchase in terms of accumulation needs to be framed differently. It needs to compare mortgage payments with the rents which would have been paid. A calculation would be made of the amount remaining, had the difference between these two figures been invested elsewhere. In addition, some adjustment would be made for maintenance and repair costs and transaction costs. These elements would need to be assessed over the lifetime and not at any particular point where they could be distorted by fluctuating items. The evaluation might indeed not be in terms of comparisons of levels of accumulation but of the pattern of rescheduling of expenditure over the life cycle. Finally, comparison between owners and renters is not the only relevant comparison. Had tenants who bought in 1973 with small discounts waited for 1980 and obtained large discounts, their position would be significantly changed depending on their changed discount entitlement and the changes in value of their home.

One further point is relevant to make in conclusion. The sitting tenant purchasers referred to in this research are of interest as a cohort well in advance of the much larger group of 1980s purchasers. Their behaviour may be taken as indicative of this later group. However, there must be some caution in assuming this to be the case - especially because of lower levels of discount, different conditions attached to purchase, and the uniformity of properties bought (no flats or acquired dwellings). However, in the absence of other data, it is appropriate to see the rates of movement and characteristics of movers as likely to be a reasonable guide to the behaviour of later council house purchasers and to the likely pattern and rate of neighbourhood change on council estates.

5 Fitting in to the market – properties after privatization

How dwellings are maintained and repaired after privatization has been touched upon in Chapter 4. It is the better built and maintained properties which tend to be sold. Consequently former council properties are generally likely to be in better condition than dwellings remaining in council ownership. If no investment in repairs and maintenance was undertaken by home owners, this comparison would change, especially where planned maintenance and capital expenditure does result in the improvement of the council stock. But one of the visible consequences of council house sales in a substantial number of cases is immediate investment in porches, fences, window replacement and wall finishings. Some of this new investment is cosmetic and symbolic and does not add to the value or utility of the dwelling as shelter. Moreover, the early rash of attractive and garish external alterations will not look so much like upgrading after ten years. There are two contrasting images of council estates affected by active investment by home owners. The first is of new roofs, extensions, porches; of the introduction of a vigorous variety and individuality into council estates and of sold properties standing out with fresh new colours and the visible impact of new investment. The second is of tired, dilapidated, shoddy porches, deteriorating paintwork and roofs and chimney stacks which stand out because they have not been replaced, while all the council owned properties around them have been reroofed and comprehensively refurbished.

The latter image does not fit with a view that council house sales will lead to greater investment in the dwelling fabric. While the original purchasers were generally affluent and were inclined to spend money on their dwellings they may not have spent it in ways which represented good investment. More importantly, their circumstances change and advancing age and declining incomes may have meant that repairs and maintenance were not sustained and may not take place again until the property changes hands on sale.

These issues are not easy to assess through research. Previous data in this book offer some examples of repairs activity but do not provide an overall picture. In order to provide a fuller picture a small exploratory house condition survey was carried on the Birmingham sample described in Chapter 1. There is no reason to believe that this sample will provide an unrepresentative picture of the condition in 1989 of council houses sold between 1968 and 1974.

Comparison of the present condition of these dwellings and those in the council stock offers a better assessment of the effects of privatization than would a comparison made at an earlier stage. After fifteen or more years the legacy of the council's practice in relation to repairs and maintenance will be less evident and that of owners more so. This will be even more true in a further ten years' time. Nevertheless, at this time the limited evidence which can be presented is the first systematic evidence available on this issue. While the small numbers involved and the form of the survey mean that data must be treated with caution, there are no better data currently available.

House Condition Survey Evidence

As part of this study, an external survey was made of 174 properties sold between 1968 and 1974 in Birmingham. These properties were those drawn on in the sample described earlier in Chapter 1. The external survey was carried out by experienced and qualified environmental health officers who had previously been involved in a survey of the condition of the Birmingham council housing stock. This survey used the same procedure and the results can be compared with those from the survey of council dwellings. An external survey of this kind is not a full survey and may not disclose a range of problems. However, carried out by qualified surveyors, it will identify key problems relating to roofs and the exterior of dwellings. These are basic to the dwellings' fabric and structural condition. Surveyors completed a pre-coded check-list relating to the dwelling and on the basis of this an indication of the costs of outstanding repairs is made.

In evaluating this evidence, comparisons are made with the council stock in Birmingham. However, in order to compare like with like in each case, all dwellings built before 1919 and all flats have been excluded. The 174 sold properties did not include any flats and only included two properties built before 1919. Hence the sample compared in the tables below is of 172 properties. The tables continue to be a comparison of what were among the best council houses with a more mixed group, but by limiting the comparison in this way this effect is less substantial. The remaining comparison can at the best only be regarded as indicative of differences.

The data obtained from this house condition survey are presented in Tables 5.1 to 5.4 and Figures 5.1 to 5.5. Table 5.1 indicates that the properties involved are of similar building method and quality. Non-traditionally built dwellings were represented in both groups but only to a slightly greater extent among existing council houses. These non-traditional building methods do not affect the quality categorization. A substantial group of former council houses were recorded as better than the representative dwelling. One factor in this is likely to be the nature and size of sites. The data on parking provision show that former council houses are significantly more likely to have parking or space for parking on the plot. Existing council homes are much more likely to depend on street parking. This conforms with the evidence that end terraces and other properties with large gardens were heavily represented in these early council house sales. Table 5.2 confirms that end terrace dwellings are disproportionately found in the 'better than representative' category.

Table 5.1
General comparisons between former and current council houses in Birmingham

	Post 1919 Dwellings Only	
	Former Council Houses	Council Houses
Sample No.	172	59601
	%	%
Building method		
Traditional	66	63
Probably traditional	3	2
Non-traditional	31	35
Quality assessment	%	%
Best of its kind	-	0.4
Better than basic	99.4	99.6
Basic	0.6	-
Is dwelling representative of adjacent dwellings?	%	%
Yes - same	82	97
Yes - better than	18	2
Yes - worse than	-	1
Parking provision for dwelling	%	%
Integral garage	2	5
Garage on plot	19	6
Parking space on plot	25	12
Garage/space elsewhere	2	5
Adequate street parking	40	60
Inadequate street parking	12	11
None	1	1

Table 5.2
Former Council Dwellings:
Dwelling type and comparison with adjacent dwellings.
Is dwelling representative of adjacent dwellings?

	Better	Same
Number	31	141
	%	%
Type of dwelling		
End terrace	39	21
Mid terrace	29	41
Semi-detached	32	38
Total better dwellings	31	

Table 5.3 presents detailed assessments of house condition and it is these data which are most important for the present study. Some fifteen years after privatization, former council dwellings were more likely to have very limited repair costs than those still in council ownership. However, they were also more likely to have repair costs in excess of £2,500. The differences in distribution of repair costs would support a view that while former council homes were generally in better condition, there is a significantly greater tendency for some properties to lag behind and fall into a relatively high repair cost category. This general pattern and the polarization implied within the former council homes category is also apparent in the assessments of external and party wall structure, yard pavings and walls, pitched roof coverings and roof drainage. The data on repair costs and wall structures are reproduced in Figures 5.1 and 5.2. The pattern indicated for external wall surfaces, external paint and external doors and windows is different. It conforms more to the 'home owners maintain their homes better' hypothesis. These data are illustrated in Figures 5.3, 5.4 and 5.5.

Table 5.3
Comparisons of Housing Condition
External Elements and Structure: Existing and Former Council Houses in Birmingham

	Post 1919 Dwellings Only	
	Former Council Houses	Council Houses
Sample No.	172	58898
	%	%
Cost of repairs (£)		
0-250	54	36
251-500	15	13
501-750	9	10
751-1000	4	6
1001-1250	1	4
1251-1500	2	5
1501-2500	3	13
2501-4000	2	5
4001 and over	12	8
External and party wall structure	%	%
Repairs needed:		
Nil	76	70
Minor (15%)	11	12
Medium (40%)	-	12
Major (75%)	2	1
Renew (100%)	11	6
External wall surface	%	%
Repairs needed:		
Nil	67	44
Minor (15%)	16	30
Medium (40%)	3	6
Major (75%)	1	2
Renew (100%)	13	17
External paint	%	%
Repairs needed:		
Nil	48	37
Minor (15%)	23	16
Medium (40%)	11	9
Major (75%)	5	8
Renew (100%)	13	31

Table 5.3 (continued)

	Post 1919 Dwellings Only	
	Former Council Houses	Council Houses
		(n = 59601)
Yard pavings and walls	%	%
Repairs needed:		
Nil	44	38
Minor (15%)	38	45
Medium (40%)	9	12
Major (75%)	3	2
Renew (100%)	6	3
Unobtainable	1	-
External doors and windows	%	%
Repairs needed:		
Nil	55	37
Minor (15%)	27	32
Medium (40%)	8	12
Major (75%)	2	4
Renew (100%)	8	14
Unobtainable	-	*
Pitched roof coverings	%	%
Repairs needed:		
Nil	75	62
Minor (15%)	16	27
Medium (40%)	1	2
Major (75%)	-	1
Renew (100%)	8	6
None/not applicable	-	2
Flat roofs	%	%
Repairs needed:		
Nil	19	17
Minor (15%)	2	2
Medium (40%)	-	*
Major (75%)	-	-
Renew (100%)	2	-
None/not applicable	77	80
Unobtainable	-	1
Roof drainage	%	%
Repairs needed:		
Nil	73	75
Minor (15%)	16	18
Medium (40%)	3	1
Major (75%)	1	-
Renew (100%)	8	6

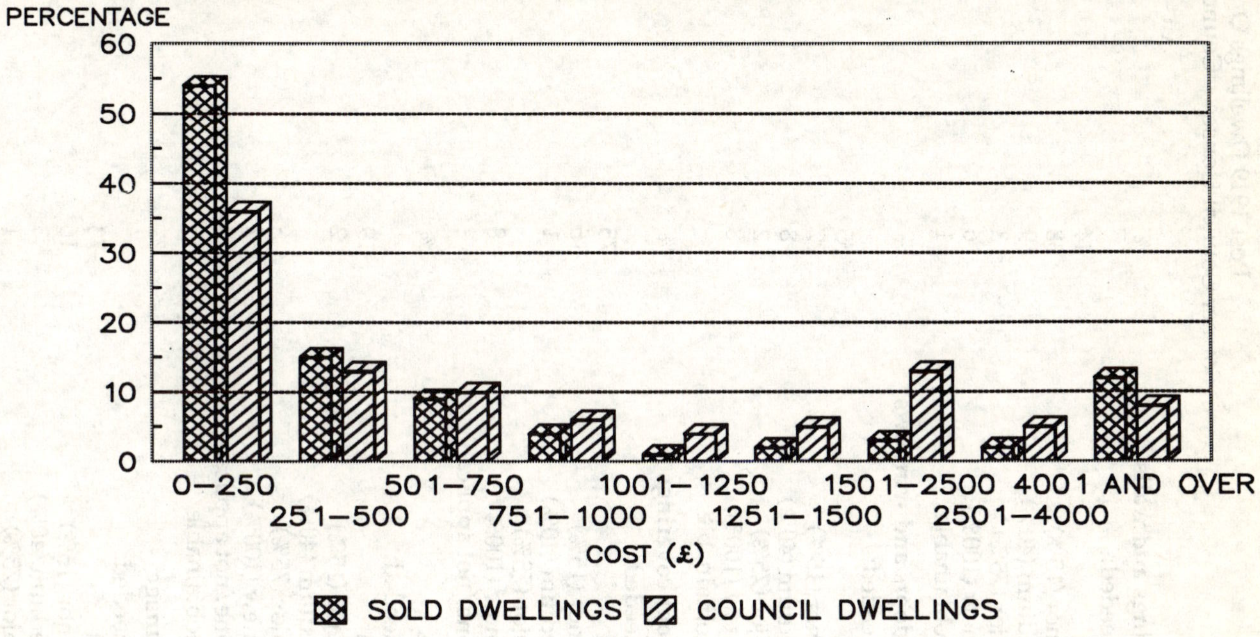

Figure 5.1 Cost of repairs - post 1919 dwellings: percentage in each category

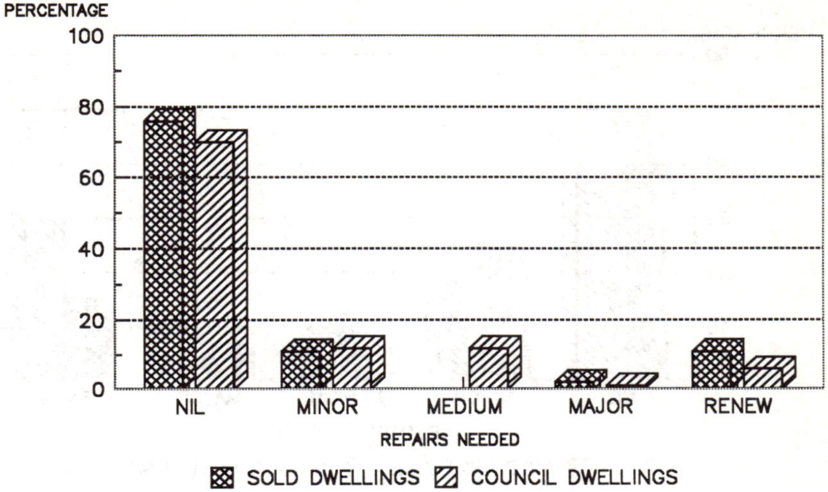

Figure 5.2 Condition of external and party wall structure

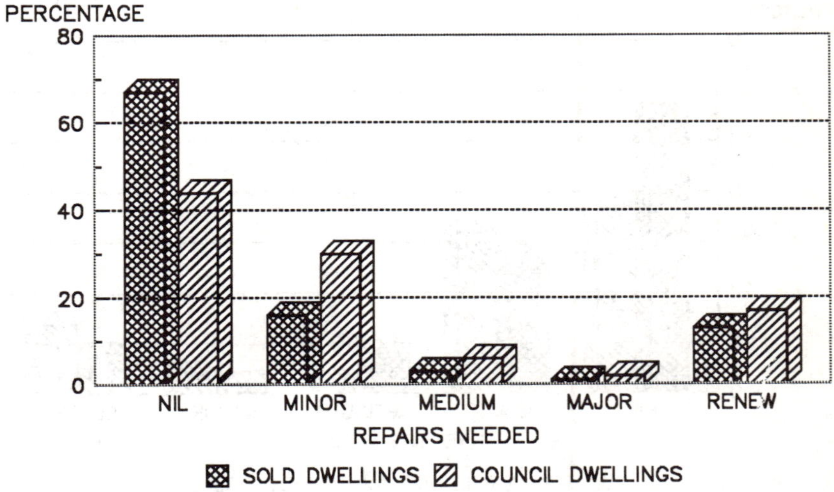

Figure 5.3 Condition of external wall surface

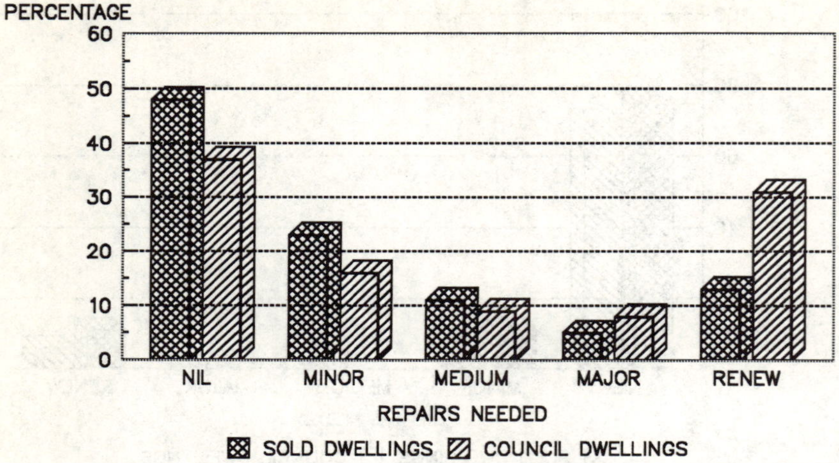

Figure 5.4 Condition of external paint

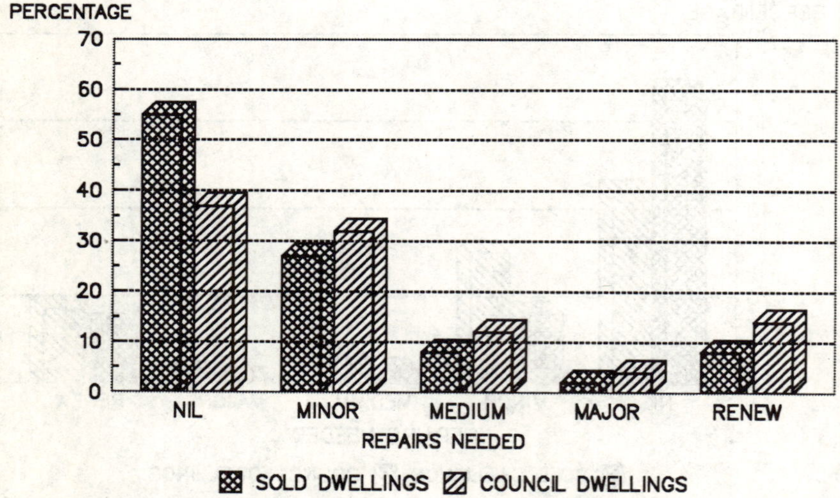

Figure 5.5 Condition of external doors and windows.

Table 5.4 provides some limited data on what appear to be the former council dwellings in worst repair. These data suggest that they tend to be post-war and semi-detached dwellings.

Table 5.4
Former council dwellings with repair costs over £1,500

	Repair Costs		
	£1501-2500	£2500-4000	£4001 and over
Total	6	3	21
Date of construction			
1900-1918	1	-	-
1919-1944	4	3	8
1945-1964	1	-	13
Post 1964	-	-	-
Type of dwelling			
End terrace	-	-	5
Mid terrace	-	2	4
Semi-detached	6	1	12

Discussion

The data presented in this chapter are limited and exploratory and must be treated with caution. They can best be regarded as raising questions which should be examined by subsequent work. This is however the only systematic evidence available to provide even an indication of the condition of former council houses after a significant period in the private sector. Fifteen or more years after sale the house condition and housing repairs profile of former council homes differs from that of existing council homes in the same city. These differences do not seem likely to reflect differences which existed at the time of initial sale. At that stage it is likely that the sold houses were of better than average condition. More than fifteen years later they were also generally in better condition. However, there is a clear indication that former council homes exhibit a wider variation of condition than council homes do. In this they reflect the fact that decisions on repairs and maintenance in the private sector will reflect individual resources and inclination. In contrast, council house repairs and maintenance decisions are bureaucratically determined following planned maintenance or refurbishment programmes as well as responding to demand. The market produces both higher standards of repair and a greater likelihood of neglect of repair. The range is wider than in the council sector. One aspect of this is that owners may accept lower standards of repair and tenants voice complaints about less severe problems. This interaction of housing tenure, professional views of house condition and users' views of house condition has been apparent in major house condition studies (DOE, 1986).

One final point of discussion is relevant in this context. The visible external alterations to dwellings which are one of the earliest and most visible consequences of privatization should not be taken as evidence of good repair or of future repair activity. Some of this visible expenditure is cosmetic and is not a substitute for more routine maintenance. And it itself requires maintenance. A rash of porches and new external wall finishes cannot be taken as evidence of superior or continuing maintenance. One possibility is that former council houses will experience periods of high maintenance expenditure especially associated with changes in ownership. As with other properties, especially cheaper properties owned by elderly and low income households, some former council houses will fall into significant disrepair. This will involve greater disrepair than in the council stock. In sum, former council homes will show a different pattern of repair than council homes and a greater range of repair and disrepair.

6 Embracing the market? – tenure attitudes of the new owners

This chapter returns to issues touched upon earlier. These are the attitudes to tenure expressed by the households interviewed in the process of the study. The study provides an opportunity to consider the views of households with direct, first hand experiences as tenant and as owner of the same dwelling. In particular this is relevant to views which present negative attitudes to council housing as a key factor in desire to purchase. This evidence relates to two broader debates. Firstly it relates to discussion of the nature of preferences for home ownership and the extent to which they are pragmatic or reflect some fundamental desire. Secondly it relates to how housing history and housing experience affect attitudes to tenure. Before presenting new evidence it is relevant to review some of the background to these debates.

Tenure Preferences

For some time data on housing tenure preferences have been treated with little respect. They have been regarded as variously flawed by post facto rationalization and by the problems inherent in asking hypothetical questions and have been felt to have little explanatory value or value in understanding people's real motivations and aspirations. Social and policy analysts have generally viewed such data as rather crude buttresses for government policies or for the promotion of a particular factional interest and hardly worthy of serious comment and consideration. Merrett (1982), for example, observed 'The existing literature on tenure preferences is marred by an excess of unstructured empiricism or ideological rubbish' (p. 56). However, in recent years, claims about consumer preferences in housing have re-emerged in rather more sophisticated forms. Within debates about the sociology of consumption (Saunders, 1986), the new consumerism or market socialism (Le Grand and Estrin, 1989) there are strong assumptions about majority preferences in housing. These preferences are commonly linked to a particular housing tenure:

> The majority own, or would like to own, capital in some form (a house, savings accounts, pension rights, insurance policies, stocks and shares). (Le Grand and Estrin, 1989, p. 23).

Market freedom and choice are explicitly equated with the unfettered individual operating in a free market. In this context, housing policy in the form of council house sales is regarded as having liberated over a million households who have been enabled to express their preference for home ownership. The 'revealed preference' for home ownership is presented as proof of basic consumer attitudes.

The fashionable reaction to the statism of much previous social analysis is a temptation to embrace the 'consumer's perspective' too easily, exclusively and uncritically. Within this new realism is a dismissal of state provision as inherently unresponsive, undesirable and repressive. People should be given what they want through the enlightened manipulation of the market. What they appear to want above almost all is an owner occupied house and it is naturally assumed that what they must passionately reject is its antithesis - council housing.

Evidence on housing tenure preferences is available for a considerable time period. Table 6.1 provides some details from the larger national surveys on the topic. Both the variation over time and the variation between regions have been commented on elsewhere (Forrest, et al., 1984). Preferences are not formed in a vacuum and reflect judgements about the quality and type of property available at any time in any tenure. They also relate to current tenure status. Except for tenants in privately rented furnished accommodation most people state a preference for the tenure they are in (Table 6.2). Thus owners prefer to own, council tenants prefer to rent from the council slightly more than they prefer to own, housing association tenants prefer that sector, tenants renting from private landlords unfurnished prefer that tenure. Against this background home ownership tends to be the second most common preference and council housing the third. This pattern of preferences may be seen as an expression of inertia. It may also be seen more positively as reflecting attachments to home and area irrespective of tenure.

Table 6.1
Current tenure and tenure preferences in two years' time (percentages)

	Estimated Tenure Distribution Great Britain				Preferred tenure (various surveys)		
	1986 %	1967 %	1975 %	1978 %	1983 %	1986 %	1989 %
Home ownership	64	66	69	72	77	77	81
Council renting	26	23	21	19	16	17	12
Private renting, housing association	10	11	8	5	5	4	3
Don't know	-	-	3	3	2	3	1

Sources: Housing and Construction Statistics and Building Societies Association, (1983); BMRB (1986); BMRB (1989).

Table 6.2
Type of accommodation would most like to live in in two years' time, according to present tenure

	Total	Buying with mortgage	Owned outright	First time buyers	Other buyers	Renting from council	Renting from Housing Asscn	Renting from Landlord furnished	Renting from Landlord unfurnished	Other
Total	2465	1128	588	477	499	545	41	60	53	27
Preferred Tenure	%	%	%	%	%	%	%	%	%	%
Owned	81	96	94	98	99	47	18	69	31	67
Rented from council	12	1	2	1	1	48	7	9	11	10
Rented from a housing asscn.	2	*	1	*	-	2	68	1	-	8
Rented from a private landlord (furnished)	1	1	1	-	-	1	-	17	3	-
Rented from a private landlord (unfurnished)	2	*	*	-	-	1	2	4	52	5
Don't know	1	1	2	1	*	1	5	-	2	10

Source: BMRB Housing and Saving 1989, p. 144.

Merrett (1982) has argued that preferences are structured according to predicates of choice. Merrett discusses six sets of attributes of dwellings which are considered in making housing choices. These are the physical character of the house, the control exercised over its use by the occupier, the attractiveness of the neighbourhood itself, the location of the neighbourhood relative to other places, the housing mobility the dwelling offers and the stream of payments and receipts associated with the possession of the home. In all of this Merrett emphasizes a framework of feasible choices and 'the pervasive influence of supply upon effective demand' (p. 57). He argues that a choice which favours owner occupation will not be based on absolute and static characteristics of a tenure but on an evaluation of what supply is available in terms of the six major attributes identified. The outcome of this evaluation will vary. Most obviously fluctuations in the financial and economic environment will tend to alter the balance of financial advantage between rental and owner occupation.

Merrett concludes that the contemporary evidence on the substantial numbers desiring to own their home rests on a clear foundation:

> Owner occupation, for households on average or higher than average wages and salaries, in general gives access to dwellings that are ranked higher in terms of their use-value and which are perceived to offer greater housing mobility and long-term financial advantages. (p. 71)

In this context it is instructive to look at other countries or at attitudes towards housing in Britain earlier in the century. For example, a study of housing by Mass Observation carried out in 1943 reveals a very different discourse about preferences and aspirations. Whilst there was a section on renting versus owning, it was far outweighed by discussion of space standards, gardens, privacy, independence and the quality of the neighbourhood. Indeed, although the discussion of the pros and cons of owning and renting has very similar dimensions to contemporary debates, tenure is given no greater importance than, say, the design of the kitchen. What is striking is how far discussion of privacy or independence and general housing quality is divorced from discussion of tenure. In contemporary literature it would be assumed by most people that the statement 'It's our own, isn't it? A home of our own' was being made by an owner occupier. Quite unremarkably for the time, it was being made by someone living in a wholly rented area (Advertising Service Guild, 1943, p. 171). And the final discussion of the 'Dream home of the future' makes no reference to home ownership. The Bournville Village Trust's study of Birmingham published in 1941 shows a similar pattern with very little discussion of ownership and an emphasis on overcrowding, rent levels, open spaces, gardens and design. The authors of the report argued that home ownership which involved buying on a mortgage under a system of weekly payments 'should really be classed with tenants who pay rent, rather than with occupiers who own their houses outright' (p. 54). The possible reasons for living in the present house, for moving and the preferences in moving did not include reference to home ownership and preference for home ownership does not appear to have been added by respondents under 'any other reason'.

These surveys were conducted during wartime when extensive bomb damage had occurred and in a period when the majority experience was of renting. They serve, nevertheless, as a reminder that in the not so distant past in Britain discussion of housing tenure was relatively unimportant. Moreover, many of the dimensions of housing which are now inextricably associated with home ownership (e.g. independence, privacy, freedom, a garden) were seen then as quite separate and no more an inherent feature of owning than of renting. Without labouring the point, it is clear that the current overwhelming preference for home ownership is not natural, inherent or cultural but reflects the current realities of the stock of dwellings, the means of access to them, the way they are managed and the financial and policy framework. If and when these circumstances change, preferences will change. It is not intended to pursue this point further here but other examples of attitudes to owning between the wars (Runciman, 1966; McCulloch, 1989) are also relevant.

An example from the National Housing Survey data for the Netherlands supports the same point. It shows a variation in tenure preferences in three years, 1977, 1981 and 1985. Among existing households who were potential movers, the proportion preferring to rent in these three years was 60.7 per cent, 72 per cent and 61.5 per cent respectively. This fluctuation was also evident among potential new households (starters), for whom the figures were 72.5 per cent, 83 per cent and 79.5 per cent respectively (Hooimeijer and Linde, 1988, p. 133). This variation relates to changes in the home ownership market and particularly the 'collapse' of home ownership in the early 1980s. Without pushing the example, it illustrates that rather than being inherent, innate, fixed or on a consistent rising trend, preferences for home ownership fluctuate and fluctuations relate to changes in the housing market.

These arguments would again suggest that there is no great value in pursuing housing tenure preferences further. However recent contributions by Saunders and Harris have reopened the topic. Saunders and Harris do not engage with the existing literature and generally prefer to argue against a position which either denies or explains away preferences for home ownership as representing false consciousness or flawed measurement. In a paper presented in 1987 they draw on their own survey evidence from interviews with council tenants and home owners in three towns. They relate their work to that of the 1986 British Social Attitudes Survey (Jowell et al., 1986) which suggests that most people in Britain favour collective consumption, and more centrally to Taylor-Gooby's (1985) conclusions that people do not see private and public modes of provision as mutually exclusive or antagonistic. Taylor-Gooby argues that people occupy a dual role in contemporary capitalist societies as both citizens and market consumers and that ideology structures popular preference and explains apparent contradictions in popular consciousness. Saunders and Harris state:

> Our survey materials support Taylor-Gooby's contention that some people express a desire for private provision while at the same time supporting the state sector universal services. Our tentative explanation for this is, however, somewhat different, for we do not see it as a function of 'commodity fetishism', but rather as the product of highly constrained effective choices. (p. 11)

Furthermore, in relation to housing, Saunders and Harris argue that the dualism thesis developed by Taylor-Gooby is misleading:

> .... for in the case of housing there is a strong and coherent majority preference for private provision....

They go on:

> In the case of housing it is quite clear that most people have a strong and consistent set of values favouring market provision against that of the state. There is little evidence here of ambivalence and dualism, nor is there any reason to believe that such a strong set of preferences is the product of ideological distortion or contamination. On the contrary it is the generally positive experience of private ownership which leads most owner occupiers so strongly to favour private housing, just as it is the often negative experience of state renting which leads most council tenants to support policies such as the Right to Buy legislation and the provision of mortgage interest tax relief which make ownership more possible, if not for them, then perhaps for their children. (p. 14)

Saunders and Harris acknowledge that in part the commitment to home ownership is a reflection of economic factors - increasing asset values in home ownership and rising rents with no asset in return - which were prominent features of housing at the time of their interviews. However the issue of autonomy and control was most frequently mentioned (in opposite ways) by both home owners and council tenants. Saunders and Harris's survey found 65 per cent of council tenants regarded their council as unresponsive as a landlord - and the demand to buy was highest (at 87 per cent) among this group. They conclude:

> What all this amounts to is that there is a high degree of dissatisfaction among tenants, and it is this rather than any ideological factor which lies at the root of their strong but often frustrated desire to 'exit' from the state sector. To adopt Barnett's metaphor, they may be hanging on the nipple of state maternalism, but the experience is far from satisfying. (p. 15)

Saunders and Harris's survey suggests that dualism in relation to housing is most evident among home owners who do not approve of council house sales and the discounts available. This feature, however, is not supported by other surveys. The 1986 British Social Attitudes Survey showed that council tenants did not differ from those in other tenures over their attitude to the Right to Buy (Jowell et al., 1986, pp. 146-8). A consistent 9 per cent of respondents across all tenures disapproved of council house sales.

Available Evidence

Saunders and Harris's view can be challenged in a number of ways. Firstly, certain assumptions appear to have coloured their interpretation of their data. For example, they present council house purchasers as in a position of constrained choice with insufficient resources to exit from the state sector and dependent on discounts to enable them to buy. These assumptions do not stand up to checks against evidence about purchasers. There is a consistent body of evidence which has established that a substantial proportion of those who buy council houses as sitting tenants could have bought houses elsewhere in the city they lived in. (For a review of this evidence, see Forrest and Murie, 1988a.) The reason that they do not relates to other aspects of neighbourhood, house and home and indicates that Saunders and Harris are wrong to imply that the 'negative', 'push' factors relating to state landlordism dominate their preferences. Indeed while they may feel that the council as a landlord is unresponsive they do not feel that this requires remedy. Saunders and Harris's implication that this may relate to consumption being experienced 'passively rather than actively' and being 'generally denied the opportunity of making decisions and resolving choices' is an unconvincing product of their own assumptions and certainly does not hold up for this group. If there is a negative push factor it seems to relate more to rent levels and expectations of continuing increases in rent. This element is consistently referred to in research evidence, (see, for example, Northern Ireland Housing Executive, 1981; Foulis, 1985; Kerr, 1988).

Secondly, and linked to this, it is appropriate to consider whether the range of questions asked by Saunders and Harris was sufficient and whether the way questions were asked and recorded affected their results to an unusual or unacceptable extent. Rather than sound like the last resort of the sceptical critic, there are some direct grounds for this view. Saunders and Harris base their conclusions on four (inevitably) far from exhaustive questions. These refer to generalized preferences for owning or renting, and statements about support or opposition to council house sales and to tax relief. Questions about preferences for owning and renting have been used in a number of surveys with differing wording and different results. The data which are available and relevant to the issues which Saunders and Harris discuss, do not form a neat, coherent set. Material about attitudes to council housing sometimes refers to attitudes to the dwelling or accommodation, sometimes to preferred tenure, sometimes to movement intentions and sometimes to satisfaction with specific aspects of the landlord service. Rather than writing this off as presenting a confused picture, this variety indicates the complexity of attitudes to tenure. The tendency is for council tenants to be generally satisfied with their dwelling, and with most aspects of landlord service, but to express a preference for home ownership. Saunders and Harris's findings of negative attitudes to council housing appear therefore to be out of step with this. Their view that support of or opposition to council house sales is a clear test of support of the statist mode also appears superficial.

Saunders and Harris's presentation of the high degree of dissatisfaction among council tenants (some 65 per cent dissatisfied) does not sit comfortably alongside responses to different questions relating to the same issue. The 1986 BMRB Survey showed 77 per cent of local authority tenants were either very satisfied (32 per cent) or fairly satisfied with their housing (BMRB, 1986). The National Dwelling and Housing Survey carried out for England in 1978 showed 26 per cent of council tenants interviewed (5,013) were very satisfied with their accommodation and 48 per cent fairly satisfied (DOE, 1978). The 1983 British Social Attitudes Survey (Jowell and Airey, 1984), showed 74 per cent of local authority tenants satisfied with their accommodation. The 1986 British Social Attitudes Survey referred to 17 per cent of council tenants dissatisfied with their present accommodation and 24 per cent preferring to buy (Jowell et al., 1986, pp. 144-5). A 1988 survey of 1,043 council tenants in Wales showed 42 per cent very satisfied and 42 per cent fairly satisfied with their dwelling (Clinton et al., 1989). A 1989 survey in England (Centre for Housing Research, 1989, p. 95) showed that 67 per cent of the 998 council tenants interviewed rated their service at least satisfactory. And the most recent survey by the Building Societies' Association (BSA, 1989) found fewer than 10 per cent of council tenants expressing dissatisfaction with their housing.

These surveys tend to refer to the dwelling rather than the tenure. But one perspective would be that attitudes to tenure are fundamentally influenced by the dwelling. The recent English and Welsh surveys (CHR, 1989; Clinton et al., 1989) do probe further into attitudes to landlord services and do indicate higher levels of dissatisfaction with various aspects of landlord service (and especially repairs). They also indicate that tenants have some awareness of the wider context in which council landlords operate. For example, only 31 per cent of tenants in the English survey believed their landlord had adequate resources for provision. One interpretation of all this is that council tenants' attitudes to tenure are much more complex and sophisticated than allowed for by Saunders and Harris. Tenants see their housing situation in a more rounded and material way. They respond to the dwelling and its facilities and security of tenure as well as (and to a greater degree than) other dimensions of housing service, rights and ontological security. The evidence from the most recent studies shows that levels of dissatisfaction among council tenants consistently relate to features of dwelling stock (age and dwelling type), urban/rural dimensions, age and other household circumstances. It suggests that attitudes to tenure are not based on abstracted representations of rights and security but on real housing experience.

In this context it is relevant also to refer to the recent spate of surveys linked to the Tenants' Choice measures introduced by the Housing Act, 1988. A MORI poll commissioned by Manchester City Council in 1988 indicated that if tenants had a choice of landlord, the majority would prefer to remain council tenants. If the choice was between the council and a tenants' co-operative, 55 per cent would opt for the council (20 per cent don't know). If the choice was between the council and a private landlord 88 per cent would opt for the council (8 per cent don't know). A survey commissioned by the National Consumer Council in 1988 (Gallup, 1988), provided a similar picture of strong support for local authority control and very limited support for private landlordism. Other polls in Peterborough and Thamesmead produced similar results (City of Peterborough, 1986; 1987; London Housing News, 1988). However, ballots in Chiltern, Sevenoaks, Newbury, South Wight, Medina, Rochester, Swale, North Bedfordshire, Mid Sussex and Broadland all produced majorities of tenants in favour of voluntary transfers to housing associations. Other ballots in Ynys Mon, Rochford, Salisbury, Torbay, Arun, Three Rivers, Brentwood, Redbridge and Elmbridge produced majorities against. Evidence from a small survey of some 600 predominantly working class households in three towns is also relevant to this debate (Forrest and Murie, 1988b). A sub-section of the questionnaire referred to attitudes towards various public/private alternatives in service provision. The sample was drawn from council and owner occupied areas associated with different qualities of housing. The general message from this survey is that support for council house sales and for transfers of management of council housing do not go hand in hand. Different forms of privatization generate different levels of support (Table 6.3). While there is consistent and substantial support for council house sales, opinion is much more divided on the transfer of management functions from council to private or quasi-public landlords. Tenants in the worst council housing are most in favour of sales and least in favour of management transfers.

Table 6.3
Attitudes to council house sales and management transfers

	All Respondents	Council Housing Areas		Owner Occupied Areas	
		Good	Bad	Good	Bad
	%	%	%	%	%
Approve council house sales	78	79	80	75	79
Disapprove	14	15	12	13	17
Indifferent	5	5	2	2	1
No opinion	1	1	2	9	1
Don't know	2	1	4	1	3
Approve transfer of management of council housing	35	37	28	39	38
Disapprove	36	36	45	28	39
Indifferent	10	11	6	16	9
No opinion	7	9	4	8	3
Don't know	11	7	17	9	11

Source: Authors' household survey in Consett, Cheltenham and Accrington

Considerable caution is required in generalizing from such data. But the evident support for individual sales is fully consistent with a view that dissatisfaction with council house management cannot be 'read off' from support for council house sales. Tenants may desire substantial improvements in the quality of service they receive from the council but they do not necessarily believe that the solution lies in the privately rented sector or through transferring from a large municipal landlord to a housing association.

In simple terms, this sort of evidence is compatible with a view that those households who remain in the public rented sector desire the benefits of home ownership associated with greater user control and better housing quality; a majority do not wish to buy their current dwelling; and alternative forms of landlordism do not offer such a future. The conclusion from this evidence is that while there is some demand to change landlord, this is not substantial and is not the principal preoccupation of council tenants. There is no desire for transfer to private landlords. This does not eliminate the possibility that attractive, persuasive packages could be put together to alter this view. Attitudes to tenure will change in response to such packages and are not static and culturally determined.

Saunders and Harris's perception of housing choices and decisions is preoccupied with tenure and is based on a view that responses to simple questions about housing tenure will be based on common understandings and knowledge of tenure. But this is not the case. Research on housing histories shows that many households have not experienced both home ownership and council housing. When they are asked opinions about tenure they tend to refer to their own experience rather than general attitudes to tenures (Forrest and Murie, 1985; 1987). It has been argued that housing strategies reflect the housing practices learned and shared through social networks and communities. Differences in attitudes to debt, house condition, self-provisioning, landlord responsibilities and the advantages of buying a house at any particular stage reflect these practices. The recent debate about home centredness and privatism has tended to emphasize continuity in housing practices in spite of changing tenure structures (Franklin, 1989). Tenure led explanations have not proved robust in this environment and it is appropriate to develop a picture of housing preferences based on different models.

Alternative Evidence

In the remainder of this chapter evidence from a survey of households in a particular part of the housing market is presented to develop an alternative to Saunders and Harris's view of the relationship between attitudes to council housing and home ownership. The intention in this is not to assert the correctness of data from research which suffers from many of the same methodological problems faced by Saunders and Harris. Rather it is to suggest that tenure preferences are more complicated statements relating to housing history and experience and other attributes of dwellings and localities. They are more likely to be the output of housing decisions than to be the key inputs determining housing choices.

Evidence from the study of households who purchased their dwellings from the council between 1968 and 1973 is relevant in this context. A series of attitudinal questions relating to tenure was included in this study. The 244 original tenant purchasers, five successors and 167 open market purchasers had very different experiences to draw upon in making assessments of tenure. Furthermore the open market purchasers group (more than 90 per cent of whom knew that the house involved had been a council house) included households who had experience as council tenants. From this the sample can be subdivided as follows:

(a) Sitting tenant purchasers with an experience of council housing fifteen or more years previously

Birmingham	134
London	110

(b) Open market purchasers who had some prior experience of living in council housing

Birmingham	20
London	35

(c) Open market purchasers who were tenants immediately before buying their present house

Birmingham	13
London	28

Tables 6.4 and 6.5 list the responses to a series of questions on attitudes to council housing. These are the same data as presented earlier, in Chapter 2, but now more fully disaggregated. Some caution should be exercised over the smaller sample numbers for open market purchasers. Nevertheless, a number of impressions emerge. Sitting tenant purchasers, looking back on their experience as council tenants do not generally express negative views. Eighty-five per cent of those in London and 79 per cent in Birmingham were either very satisfied or fairly satisfied with their experience of the council as landlord. These percentages are widely different from those of Saunders and Harris. Both this and Saunders and Harris's study reflect preferences and views developed in different contexts. In this study of former council tenants those expressing dissatisfaction with specified aspects of service never form a majority. There are particularly high levels of satisfaction over the 'quality of accommodation'. The lowest levels of satisfaction are expressed in relation to 'ability to move or get a transfer' 'freedom to do what you wanted with the property' and 'security if your home circumstances changed'. Most significantly in relation to Saunders' preoccupations are the high proportion of households expressing positive views over feeling the council house was their own home.

The picture for open market purchasers is different. The high proportion of responses not expressing an opinion confuses the picture. Nevertheless a higher proportion of this group expressed a negative view of their experience of council housing. Again quality of accommodation generated more positive responses. The most negative responses were not over 'feeling that the house was your own home' but over 'ability to move or get a transfer' and, to a lesser extent, 'freedom to do what you wanted with the property'. Open market purchasers with direct experience of council housing immediately before buying their present house present a more polarized picture than those whose experience is less direct.

Table 6.4
'Looking back on your experience as a council tenant before you bought this house, what was your general feeling about the council as a landlord?'

	London	Birmingham
Sample No.	110	134
	%	%
Very satisfied	36	31
Fairly satisfied	49	48
Neither	7	6
Fairly dissatisfied	3	5
Very dissatisfied	-	7
Can't remember/don't know	5	2

Table 6.5

'Looking back at your past experiences, as far as you can remember, how satisfied or dissatisfied were you with each of the following aspects of council housing in this area?'

	Sitting Tenant Purchasers		Open Market Purchasers with some experience of living in council tenancies		Purchasers with direct experience as council tenants immediately before buying their present house	
	Birmingham	London	Birmingham	London	Birmingham	London
Sample No.	134	110	20	35	16	18
'Quality of the accommodation'	%	%	%	%	%	%
Very satisfied	42	43	20	23	13	28
Fairly satisfied	49	39	65	31	44	33
Neither	1	7	-	-	-	6
Fairly dissatisfied	1	7	10	-	19	7
Very dissatisfied	3	2	5	3	19	-
Cannot remember/No opinion	3	2	-	43	6	28
'Getting repairs and maintenance done'						
Very satisfied	16	18	-	3	6	-
Fairly satisfied	40	45	45	23	19	39
Neither	10	8	5	6	6	-
Fairly dissatisfied	17	14	15	3	6	11
Very dissatisfied	12	5	20	9	25	11
Cannot remember/No opinion	5	9	15	57	38	39
'Feeling it was your own home'						
Very satisfied	33	26	15	9	19	6
Fairly satisfied	40	45	50	20	6	28
Neither	7	10	5	3	-	-
Fairly dissatisfied	14	6	15	3	38	6
Very dissatisfied	2	5	-	9	31	11
Cannot remember/No opinion	4	8	15	57	6	50

	Birmingham	London	Birmingham	London	Birmingham	London
'Rent levels'						
Very satisfied	19	25	5	3	6	11
Fairly satisfied	56	55	20	26	56	28
Neither	7	5	15	6	6	6
Fairly dissatisfied	11	4	25	3	19	6
Very dissatisfied	3	2	5	-	6	-
Cannot remember/No opinion	4	9	30	63	6	50
'Ability to move or get a transfer'						
Very satisfied	10	15	5	6	-	-
Fairly satisfied	30	34	15	9	6	-
Neither	7	13	5	3	-	11
Fairly dissatisfied	21	6	15	3	13	17
Very dissatisfied	11	5	10	14	50	22
Cannot remember/No opinion	22	26	50	66	31	50
'Freedom to do what you wanted with the property'						
Very satisfied	11	15	-	-	-	6
Fairly satisfied	34	30	25	14	19	39
Neither	6	19	10	11	6	-
Fairly dissatisfied	16	15	25	3	25	-
Very dissatisfied	27	11	10	11	31	11
Cannot remember/No opinion	5	10	30	60	19	44
'Security if your circumstances changed'						
Very satisfied	14	14	5	-	-	6
Fairly satisfied	37	39	25	23	50	33
Neither	10	14	25	9	6	-
Fairly dissatisfied	9	8	10	-	6	11
Very dissatisfied	22	3	5	6	19	6
Cannot remember/No opinion	8	23	30	63	19	44

Table 6.6

'Looking back at your experience as an owner occupier, could you please tell me how satisfied or dissatisfied you are with each of the following aspects of privately owned housing in this area?'

	Very satisfied	Fairly satisfied	Neither	Fairly dissatisfied	Very dissatisfied	Can't remember, No opinion
'Quality of the accommodation'						
London	71	24	3	2	-	1
Birmingham	61	26	1	5	4	2
'Getting repairs and maintenance done'						
London	53	27	8	3	2	7
Birmingham	48	39	1	9	2	1
'Feeling it's your own home'						
London	82	15	3	-	1	-
Birmingham	91	7	-	2	-	1
'The levels of mortgage payments'						
London	66	17	5	3	-	8
Birmingham	64	16	4	-	-	16
'Ability to move'						
London	51	22	6	3	3	15
Birmingham	60	20	5	4	6	4
'Freedom to do what you want with the property'						
London	66	26	1	3	2	2
Birmingham	82	12	2	1	2	1
'Security if your circumstances change'						
London	62	29	4	2	-	4
Birmingham	71	22	1	1	1	4

Sample Base: London: 11
Birmingham: 134

Table 6.6 summarizes responses to a series of questions similar to those previously referring to council housing but now referring to the experience of home ownership. The overwhelming impression from these data is that positive responses to home ownership are generally high and higher than previously recorded for council housing. However the pattern is not uniform and some dimensions of home ownership achieve much lower levels of 'very satisfied' and record small but important measures of dissatisfaction. The highest levels of dissatisfaction with home ownership in the area were in Birmingham where 11 per cent were dissatisfied in relation to repairs and maintenance and 10 per cent were dissatisfied in relation to problems of moving house. However these were still lower levels of dissatisfaction than those expressed on these issues in relation to council housing. The only case where dissatisfaction with home ownership was higher than with council housing was over quality of accommodation in Birmingham. This could indicate issues related to major refurbishment of council stock since sales, leaving some sold properties in less good condition than council housing in the same area.

Conclusions

The picture which emerges from these data does not deny a high demand to buy among council tenants. But it does not fit with Saunders and Harris's view that 'there is a high degree of dissatisfaction among tenants .... which lies at the root of their strong but often frustrated desire to 'exit' from the state sector' (p. 15). It would fit with a view that many households with direct experience of both tenures have positive views of *both* home ownership and council housing. Rather than issues of ownership, autonomy and control outweighing other considerations and dominating preferences and behaviour, attitudes to tenures are formed in a much more rounded and multi-dimensional way. An explanation of tenure choices and preferences need not be forced into an ideological strait-jacket or one which imposes a simple, polarized, mutually reinforcing negative/positive view of tenures. For some households the experience of council housing is negative and for some it is positive. In both cases different aspects of the experience of council housing come together in different levels of general approval. But even where strong positive attitudes exist there may be preferences and decisions to buy. For sitting tenant purchasers discount and cost factors and the capacity to buy their home rather than just another house results in too good an opportunity to be missed. The picture is not one of desperately seeking to exit or to own. Tenure is only one of the dimensions of housing which households bear in mind in making decisions. Where the opportunity exists to satisfy a number of dimensions households will respond to opportunities in a consistent, coherent way reflecting their resources and the framework of constraints. Where tenure change could only be achieved by forgoing some other valued aspect of housing, it is not as important as Saunders implies and (for those with choice) does not necessarily mean moving.

This perspective on preferences for tenure is compatible with Merrett's general predicates and with a wider literature on housing mobility and choice which Saunders tends to neglect or dismiss. However, it is possible to go further than this. Merrett's framework stresses objective characteristics and evaluations of alternatives. He acknowledges that the diversity of needs and household compositions will be reflected in the evaluation of dwellings and offers long lists of influences relating to family, lifestyle and activity. It may be that some of these elements should be given more prominence alongside Merrett's predicates. In this it is relevant to note that Merrett tends to construct his model around newly formed households and those embarking on independent use of housing for the first time. For established households there may be different key elements. Most obviously the strength of attachment to existing home and opportunities to exercise choices within that home could be understated if the new household is in focus. It may be argued that inertia or attachment to existing home are merely elements in the evaluation of key attributes. However, an alternative is to give more prominence to current housing satisfaction, housing experience and housing practices. Whether and how people plan their housing strategies and review their housing situation and what assumptions their experience and that of family and friendship networks leads them to adopt are important. So are the resources and constraints which derive from employment and employer rather than direct income. The research reported here points to the importance of housing, family and job history. It does not support a picture of tenure choice and preference deriving either from ideological pressures, a natural desire to own or preferences constructed around tenure itself rather than a wider agenda of housing concerns. Differences, say over the strength of positive or negative attitudes to council housing, are not necessarily aberrations, ideologically based contradictions or the products of fatalism, constrained choice or culturally determined stances but are reflections of real housing experience.

Such a perspective is compatible with Saunders and Harris's data, with the data presented above and with a range of evidence on residential mobility. Saunders and Harris's own formulation is not, however, compatible with the same range of evidence. Tenure preferences, however, are not created in a vacuum and changing preferences reflect individuals' interpretations of their own experience in a specific social, economic and policy context. It is in this way that preferences and choices are formed. They are not 'natural' or reflections of a desire to own irrespective of context. Housing tenure preferences are formed around experience and expectations and will reflect assumptions about what different tenures provide. Aspects of house condition, size, availability of gardens, location and return on investment are regarded differently in different areas and according to experience. This kind of perspective on attitudes to tenure and decisions to move and to buy among council tenants is more compatible with the available evidence from the national and local surveys referred to earlier. It offers a way of reconciling how some council tenants can express high levels of satisfaction with council housing, little enthusiasm for alternative landlords, a preference for home ownership, yet at the same time take advantage of opportunities to buy as sitting tenants but show a lack of enthusiasm for moving in order to buy.

Perspectives which offer a simple interpretation of 'exiting' from the state sector as a response to dissatisfaction with state housing provision misunderstand and misrepresent the history of council house sales policy and neglect the context within which such choices are made. More serious, however, is the neglect of the role of state housing in providing the stepping stone or preconditions for satisfactory entry to home ownership. Too much of the contemporary literature on housing provision specifically or on state provision in general presents highly polarized views of council housing and home ownership. For many households the experience of council housing and home ownership has not been oppositional. On the contrary, access to state housing has played a crucial enabling role in a housing market with developing problems of affordability. Rather than viewing over a million council house sales as a mass exit from an unpopular tenure, it is more accurately represented as a mass entry to a market which could not satisfy aspirations without the existence of a large stock of high quality state dwellings. To neglect that reality in current debates about consumerism and market socialism risks erecting grand theory on flimsy and debatable assumptions about housing tenure preferences. As has been shown, the evidence on housing tenure preferences remains highly questionable. These problems are, however, compounded if the available evidence is used selectively and uncritically.

Finally, there are conclusions to be drawn from a discussion of a particular policy area for the general treatment of preferences for different modes of provision. Simple assertions about majority preferences for ownership can too easily misrepresent the various dimensions of preference formation and offer reductionist perspectives with apparent policy implications which take little account of the real feelings of consumers.

7 After the revolution – council estates after privatization

Introduction

This book has been concerned principally with the longer term effects of council house sales as former council dwellings and former council tenants filter into the private market. After ten years of the Right to Buy over a million council dwellings have been sold. We have argued elsewhere that any evaluation of the policy must be situated in a wider context which acknowledges both broader patterns of social change and the overall shape of housing policy at particular times (Forrest and Murie, 1988a). In other words, there are no inherent or inevitable consequences which flow from transferring dwellings from the state to the private market. The consequences depend upon a range of factors including when and where the dwellings were sold; who bought them; what else is happening in the housing market at the same time; whether they are being replaced in any form; as well as more profound societal changes in relation to patterns of employment and unemployment, social and spatial differentiation and changes in links between housing tenure and other aspects of social status.

Before embarking on a discussion of some of the theoretical and policy issues raised in the previous chapters it is appropriate to make a few observations about the dwellings and households which have been the focus of this study. First, as we have stressed elsewhere, we have sampled purposively some of the best examples of public sector housing. The main reason for this was to explore the impact of sales on social and spatial mobility for those households in the most advantageous position in the council sector. Another reason was to provide some necessary balance to the dominant contemporary image of public sector housing - unpopular flats or houses in inner urban or peripheral locations. A second consideration concerns the conditions in which those dwellings were sold. Compared to the Right to Buy sales of the 1980s, discounts were much lower, purchasers were uniformly more affluent and typically more concentrated at a particular stage in the family life cycle and the economic and political context was very different. The 1968-73 period did, however, see high house price inflation comparable to the early to mid-'eighties and then, as now, that inflation had strong regional variations. Thirdly, we have sampled sales in areas of London and Birmingham. Whilst strong contrasts do emerge as regards the role played by former council dwellings in the two housing markets and in terms of property appreciation, even greater contrasts would have emerged between, say, Camden and Accrington. There are a number of reasons therefore why we cannot generalize from the results of this study, spatially or temporally, without qualification. Nevertheless, the fundamental process of the absorption into the owner occupied market of dwellings previously owned and allocated by the state through bureaucratic processes will not differ. The precise consequences of that process, however, will be contingent on a range of factors which have been referred to previously. Moreover, whilst the findings from this study are about sales of a particular set of dwellings to a particular group of tenants under specific circumstances, they enable us to confront generalizations made by others about policy consequences and wider implications.

Key Findings

What are the principal empirical results from this study? First of all, a substantial number of the purchasing households in this research have not moved. After fifteen-twenty years, around 60 per cent are still in the same dwellings they bought from the council. When questioned on various aspects of home ownership they show high levels of satisfaction and have few if any regrets about the choice they made. Equally, however, their recollections of being council tenants are by no means ones of alienated dissatisfaction. On the contrary, they emerge as being highly satisfied with most aspects of the service. On these findings it is evident that 'exiting' from the state sector through sitting tenant purchase cannot be interpreted as simply being about dissatisfaction with council housing. There is no paradox in being highly satisfied with a council tenancy but taking advantage of generous terms of purchase. A greater paradox would be mass sales to dissatisfied tenants. This may increasingly happen if tenants' decisions to purchase become more strongly influenced by an uncertain financial and management environment in the state sector. Some tenants who are living in dwellings they would not have chosen to purchase or who are at a stage in the family life cycle where home ownership may not be the most appropriate tenure, may well choose to exit from the state sector. In such a situation however movement out of the state sector is being structured and manipulated by legislative and policy change. To interpret sitting tenant purchase under any circumstances as being a simple expression of disillusionment or dissatisfaction with state housing is erroneous. It is certainly the case that in the sample of early purchasers there are those who are negative about certain aspects of state provision, particularly repairs and maintenance. Equally, however, satisfaction with the quality of the dwelling or with housing costs is very high. Interpretation of questions of satisfaction with council housing needs to be precise about what aspects of the service are being evaluated. Among the early purchasers a survey of tenure preferences would no doubt have revealed a strong desire for home ownership. Many of them could, however, have moved from the state sector and bought elsewhere in the private market. And in Birmingham a relatively affluent set of council tenants would not have faced major difficulties of affordability in the owner occupied sector. That they chose not to do so indicates that tenure was not the overriding consideration for them. Moreover, the fact that after more than fifteen years the majority had remained in the same dwellings in the same areas demonstrates that discounted purchase was the icing on the cake rather than making the difference between a satisfactory and unsatisfactory housing situation.

Another important set of findings concerns resales. The evidence from this study consolidates the results of an earlier postal survey of resales (Forrest, 1980). Those who buy former council dwellings are more comparable to first time buyers in general and are more affluent than new council tenants and applicants for new council housing. They are not drawn overwhelmingly from a group of potential renters. There is no evidence that as former council dwellings enter the pool of dwellings for sale on the open market they extend opportunities for purchase down the income structure. What they appear to offer is good value for money for a group of households who would have bought elsewhere in the market. It is only possible to speculate on the potential filtering effect of this process. For example, households who buy former council dwellings might have otherwise chosen to buy an older terraced house. Such terraced dwellings may therefore be more easily available to lower income households as they are pushed down market. This effect may be more evident in some local housing markets than in others, for instance Birmingham rather than London. Where sales have occurred on a substantial scale such a process could generate a pool of lower priced dwellings available to lower income households. It remains a matter of debate whether, in the current financial and policy climate the purchase of a low value dwelling requiring often substantial investment is necessarily a good option for households with limited resources.

A further aspect of the resale process which emerges from these data and which differs from the earlier Birmingham evidence is the high number of second time buyers. In the London sample almost half of the open market purchasers (47 per cent) had previously owned a dwelling. Such evidence indicates that in London at least former council houses are not adding a new layer to the bottom end of the private housing market. Given the size and quality of the dwellings sold this is hardly surprising yet it remains a commonly expressed belief about the subsequent impact of council house sales.

The most difficult area to investigate has been the destinations of households who have moved on after they bought their dwellings. The tracing of households is an expensive and time consuming process. In our assessment of this aspect we have been able to compare the profile of the original Birmingham purchasers with those who moved. We have also discussed individual case studies of a small number of households who were traced to their next dwelling. Some of the methodological issues in tracing are elaborated in the Appendix. Needless to say our findings and conclusions from these data are more tentative.

In comparing the original Birmingham sample with the moving cohort it seems that those who had moved on tended to be either younger or older than the sample as a whole. In other words, households in the family growth stage had a higher propensity to move. And households at or nearing retirement were more likely to move to other more suitable dwellings. Those in the reduction stage, where children were growing up and were leaving home were more likely to have stayed where they were. The suggestion that family life cycle factors played an important part in the overall pattern of turnover was also evident from the case studies. Equally, some households had grown dissatisfied with the area in which they had bought or job reasons had forced a move. In one case, household dissolution through divorce had necessitated movement. There was, however, little evidence of households pursuing an explicit investment strategy of high mobility generated by a desire to move to an area where housing appreciation would be greater. There were households who had experienced a high level of accumulation from their housing moves whose council house purchase had proved to be an excellent investment. And there were others where the gains had been less dramatic or very marginal. The pattern of differential accumulation (Forrest and Murie, 1989) and the explanation for different housing market trajectories were linked more to job history than housing history. In examining the current housing circumstances of some of the original purchasers it could be assumed that their position was the product of purchasing their council dwellings. Over the whole sample, however, it is evident that labour market position and labour market processes are of equal if not greater importance in shaping individual housing histories (for a more general discussion see Forrest and Murie, 1987). A by-product of job imperatives may well be substantial accumulation through the housing market. Cause and effect can, however, be easily confused.

The evidence on the physical condition of dwellings presented in Chapter 5 has to be treated with some caution. Nevertheless, it is the only systematic evidence available on this aspect of tenure conversion through council house sales. What it indicates is that home owners do look after their properties better. Much of the repairs, maintenance and improvement activity appears, however, to be cosmetic rather than concerned with the basic fabric of the dwelling. It also appears that among those properties which have been transferred there is a greater degree of contrast in house condition. The new owners may range from the enthusiastic improvers to the highly neglectful. What this suggests for the future of such estates is a greater mixture of housing standards and maintenance activity. As home ownership comes to dominate previously council owned estates so improvement activities will be more uneven and sporadic compared to the planned and other maintenance activities of the local authority. Such estates may become more reminiscent of inner city areas with much greater contrasts between dwellings in terms of refurbishment and repair.

What do the data suggest for where former council homes will fit into the housing market? The prices realized by the most marketable sectors of the council stock vary considerably especially between London and Birmingham. Less marketable properties and properties in different markets will realize different prices. Some dwellings built with precast reinforced concrete and of non-traditional construction may have very low values, reflecting a reluctance of financial institutions to regard them as security for a loan. Other acquired dwellings indistinguishable from other private sector dwellings may, in the right location, attract very high prices. The market value of former council properties is important because it determines whether households which obtain council housing would be able to afford to buy former council homes on the open market. The prices of individual dwellings are likely to reflect three elements in turn.

(i) Regional/district price ranges reflecting levels of demand prevailing in the housing market. The prevailing level of house prices will reflect the local labour market and income levels.

Within that framework:

(ii) The estate and neighbourhood - location, design, layout, reputation, the extent of privatization, whether the area appears private or retains dwelling types (flats and maisonettes) associated with council housing, open space and estate layout;

and within this:

(iii) Dwelling characteristics - type of individual dwelling design, size, construction, faults, site details, garage, garden, heating system, energy conservation.

In this sense the prices commanded by former council homes are likely to relate to those obtaining in the local housing market. Very similar dwellings will command different prices in different localities. These prices, except for dwellings with exceptional characteristics, are likely to be within the affordability of households trading up within home ownership or with more than one wage earner or with substantial household income. But those not in employment are not likely to be able to buy. And some properties on some estates will have moved, with the market, beyond the reach of ordinary families within whose reach they previously were as council dwellings. As privatization proceeds and dwellings and estates are more fully embraced within the market more and better dwellings will move further beyond the reach of such households. They will depend either on the residual rented sectors or on lower quality properties whose prices rise less quickly precisely because demand is siphoned off by better quality former council houses.

Two final elements are likely to affect this. The first is the overall fluctuation or volatility of the private market. The second is the management of the process of market integration by exchange professionals. Without labouring this latter point, it is possible that the operation of the housing market is strongly influenced, especially in an adjustment of the type discussed here, by the opinions, advice and market making of key professional groups. Moving the market may be slower if such groups continue to label properties as council properties and to advise customers that this reduces price and demand compared with other properties. Such advice may talk this sector of the market down or slow its integration with the rest of the market.

Discussion

Earlier it was stressed that to embark on an evaluation of the pros and cons of selling state dwellings would be a rather pointless endeavour. This ground is now well trodden and the policy is well established. There is no suggestion, however, that the empirical evidence and the detailed assessments of the policy consequences are somehow flawed. On the contrary most of the predictions about the social and spatial consequences have been proved to be accurate as the policy has progressed and gathered momentum. In this study we have however sought to move beyond the shorter term and immediate impacts and to reflect on some of the wider issues involved. And in those terms the questions raised by the sale of state dwellings and their subsequent resale on the open market are by no means exhausted.

Housing tenure and housing histories

What then of the future after privatization? Have the circumstances and outlooks of those tenants who bought been so radically transformed through tenure change? What does our evidence contribute to understanding the changing social structure of Britain and the widely discussed division in social consumption? What is the likely impact of the privatization of state housing on patterns of residential differentiation and neighbourhood change?

The literature across a range of disciplines acknowledges the significance of council house sales in the changing social and economic fabric of Britain over the past decade. In Britain the proportion of dwellings in home ownership grew from 56 per cent to 66 per cent in the 1980s. And the sale of council dwellings has been the major element in that growth. The policy has had a direct and important impact on a large number of working class households and the significance of home ownership status is at the centre of sociological debates regarding the social and political transformations of Thatcherism (Marshall et al., 1988; Saunders, 1990; Pahl and Wallace, 1988).

Without elaborating on what has become an extensive debate (see for example Pratt, 1982; Forrest, 1983; Murie, 1986; Sullivan, 1989), it is worth pointing out that 'public' and 'private' have tended to be overpolarized in these discussions - as have images of home ownership and council housing. In reality there is a much greater blurring at the edges with council house sales being a prime example of the way in which 'private' destinations are the product of the shaping of housing histories through forms of state provision. Moreover, in general, the section of the working class who have benefited from these policies are the skilled manual workers who have been in an historically powerful economic position. It is evident, therefore, that their current consumption location is intimately connected to their historical position in the labour market. In a similar way, the housing histories of senior executives and professionals at the top end of the market are shaped by a distinct set of processes associated with their organizational careers in particular sectors and internal markets (Forrest and Murie, 1987).

The need to explore questions of access and the specificity of housing histories is taken up in a recent paper by Sullivan (1989). She suggests that:

> .... what has to be explained relates not so much to the fact that housing tenure currently 'cross cuts' the social classification, but rather the process whereby the 'labour aristocracy' have been absorbed into consumption locations which historically have been more often associated with the upper and middle classes. Put more generally, this involves the study of the processes whereby individuals gain access to particular consumption sector locations. (p. 186)

In this context, council house sales have been of considerable importance and have represented a very particular means of access for a section of the working class. Sullivan is correct to assert that we should be less concerned with current tenure patterns and their relationship to class locations, and pay greater attention to processes of stratification in the housing market. Doing so will expose the links between differential power in the labour market and differentiated routes of access in the housing market. The working class households discussed in this paper have a particular experience of home ownership because of their particular experience of state housing. There is not a sharp break between the two. One of Haddon's (1970) key criticisms of Rex and Moore's (1967) original formulation of housing classes was that households in the same segment of the housing market at a particular moment could be on widely differing trajectories. Such a critique remains pertinent to contemporary debates about mass home ownership and applies more generally to origins and destinations in the housing market. In exploring current tenure divisions, we need to take account of trajectories over a lifetime. Those lifetime experiences may shape people's attitudes towards and experiences of home ownership or council housing. And those housing market experiences are shaped in important ways by the world of work and cannot be seen simply in terms of processes in the sphere of consumption.

One thing is clear, within this new phase of privatized consumption, the hierarchy of housing circumstances and conditions corresponds more closely to income position. The crude, and mostly inaccurate, caricatures of Jaguar driving, affluent council tenants so often described by right wing politicians in the 1960s and 1970s pointed nevertheless to a real dislocation between home ownership status, housing quality and ability to pay. A large number of public tenants enjoyed the use value of a relatively inexpensive, high quality house and whatever the economic rationale they were disinclined to move simply to change tenure status - especially when that move could have involved a reduction in living standards. The creaming off of the best dwellings and more affluent tenants has re-established the normal order of things whereby the poorest sections in society have access only to the worst housing. Those who can buy enter the private market and establish their position in the social hierarchy according to income and labour market status. In this changed order the ideology of the market is reinforced. State housing is increasingly associated with poor quality dwellings and poor people. The normal aspirations of consumers can then only be realized in the market place.

Neighbourhood change and residential differentiation

Council house sales can be seen as an increasingly important element in the transformation of the social structure of neighbourhoods and broad patterns of residential differentiation. The literature on social change and tenure conversion has been concerned mainly with the longstanding decline of private landlordism and the gentrification of previously privately rented areas to middle class enclaves of home ownership. This process is well documented by Hamnett and Randolph (1988) in the context of the decline of institutional landlordism in London. That study and other earlier accounts (see, for example, Cullingworth, 1963) stress the critical role of supply side factors in reshaping tenure patterns and transforming neighbourhoods. Landlords had generally underinvested and undermaintained properties. The actual and imagined problems of rent control and the privileged financial position of home ownership speeded the process. Put simply, home owners were willing to pay more than the landlords' rent income justified. And landlords preferred to put their cash elsewhere. This process of tenure change contributed to a pattern of social change which gathered pace as properties were exchanged on the open market. The initial impact was slow and uneven because many of the sales had been to sitting tenants. It was estimated that in the early 1960s some 700,000 households had bought their accommodation from private landlords as sitting tenants (DOE, 1977). Some neighbourhoods of predominantly privately rented housing were also blighted, red-lined or insulated from full market integration to some degree by the activities of public and private sector agencies. However, as open market sales gathered pace so lower income, older and working class households were replaced in these neighbourhoods by those from middle class, higher income and younger groups. Some of this succession involved a displacement of lower income households and some reflected general demographic and social change.

To what extent are there similarities between the process of tenure conversion associated with the decline of private landlordism and the sale of council houses? It would be premature and inaccurate to talk about gentrification of council estates although that possibility clearly exists in the future and has already occurred with the sale of whole blocks in inner London. Moreover, it would be a rather different form of gentrification from that described by Smith and Williams (1986) as 'the rehabilitation of working-class and derelict housing and the consequent transformation of an area into a middle-class neighbourhood' (p. 1).

It would be different to the extent that the properties transferred to owner occupation from the state sector are not swathes of 19th century dwellings requiring refurbishment (although one may speculate as to the maintenance and repair futures facing some of these properties). They are not the cast-offs from a disinvesting landlord class but the product of a central government eager to cash in on generally valuable, well-maintained assets. It would be different also, because the process of neighbourhood change on these estates has not been set in train by the micro decisions of individual private developers, landlords and households (albeit sustained and encouraged by the prevailing regime of housing tax reliefs and subsidies), but directly through state intervention. And it would contrast with other forms of gentrification because the neighbourhoods being transformed would not be inner city terraces or warehouse conversions on the dockside. Generally, the properties which have been transferred from the state sector are in the inner and outer suburbs - and the estates where sales are highest are the suburban ones.

And the low sale, low value, difficult to sell areas are in the inner city or isolated on the outer peripheries. These are the neighbourhoods which received households displaced by slum clearance in a previous phase of redevelopment. Inner city slums which became 'rough' council estates are most likely to remain as council housing for the poor and reflect on the image of council housing, council tenants and state intervention.

There will be no rapid transformation of the majority of council estates. Some smaller estates, for example in more rural areas, may change their role and social composition relatively quickly. More likely, however, is a gradual process of market integration and assimilation as turnover occurs and new residents move in. That process of market integration will again be uneven with disinvestment and negative labelling of some former council owned estates paralleling a substantial revalorization and changed social composition of others. Council housing is not a standard product and even in design and locational terms there is substantial variation which will affect the pattern and nature of demand for ex-council houses. In some cases properties which are indistinguishable from adjacent private sector dwellings have been acquired by local authorities from builders at times of recession in the housing market. Other properties have been acquired for modernization and refurbishment. Properties of this kind are likely to be absorbed into the general pool of houses in the owner occupied market relatively quickly and easily and will command relatively high house prices.

A basic similarity between tenure conversion associated with private renting and the disposal of state owned dwellings through council house sales is the opening up of previously working class areas to competition from other social classes. This is unambiguously the case with council housing whereas the process of invasion and succession in private renting took different forms at different times. Arguably, when the vast majority of households rented from private landlords the pattern of residential differentiation had clear class dimensions. It was in the post-war period, as the private rented sector declined further, that the residue of inner city private renting became associated increasingly with working class populations. As home ownership began to encroach into these areas institutional lending criteria often excluded certain property types (e.g. the house with no front garden). But the labelling of whole areas as high risk (explicitly or as evident from investment patterns) because of the mix of property types is merely an obfuscation of the underlying discriminatory criteria - namely that certain areas of the city are regarded as bad investments because of their class or ethnic composition. And this class composition does indeed make them more vulnerable to redevelopment and/or further disinvestment.

When it comes to the assimilation of formerly state owned dwellings into the market the essential class dimension of residential differentiation is overt (see Harvey, 1989, for a theoretical account of the class basis of residential differentiation). Unlike the transfers from the privately rented sector, the state housing which has become owner occupied has not suffered from years of disinvestment and neglect. Indeed, in terms of space standards, design and location a substantial number are highly desirable dwellings. The valuation gap between ex-council houses and their private sector equivalents, the labelling of areas of council housing and ex-council housing as less desirable, is unambiguously related to issues of class and ethnicity. Class and racial stereotyping labels them as the less respectable parts of the city. By and large, in the short to medium term they are not ripe for invasion by the middle classes. As regards the initial tenure conversion, however, the investment risk has been effectively removed through the substantial discounts on offer by the state to the sitting tenants.

In the short to medium term the distributional impact of tenure conversion through council house sales is most likely to involve a redistribution of housing opportunities within the working class. Ex-council houses will remain at the bottom end of local housing markets in terms of price. They are likely to add to the range of choice available to more affluent council tenants, ex-council tenants and other working class households who can afford to buy. Conversely, those who cannot afford to buy will have less choice available and will be channelled increasingly into the least popular, most stigmatized neighbourhoods. But this distributional pattern will vary. In the short term local patterns of demand and local price contours will affect the market for ex-council houses. In highly pressurized, high demand areas middle class households may choose to buy former state owned dwellings although this form of demand will be concentrated in particular neighbourhoods. In more depressed housing markets, however, without major problems of affordability, council estates will remain firmly as working class neighbourhoods.

In speculating on these changes to the council sector we are speculating well into the future. Apart from some rapidly gentrifying enclaves of, for example, inner London, there is unlikely to be a dramatic or immediate transformation in the social role and composition of council estates. Generally we are looking ahead at least twenty or thirty years. The need for such a time horizon partly explains the reason for this study. Looking back on council house sales which occurred up to twenty years ago we are perhaps able to speculate on the likely future of estates which have experienced sales in the more recent past. As we have stressed elsewhere, however, policy details and the social and economic environment have changed substantially and it would be rash to assume that the pattern of social and neighbourhood change associated with earlier disposals from the state sector will be replicated with Right to Buy sales. A basic continuity will remain, however, in the assimilation into the general housing market of previously working class areas of housing which were isolated from housing market processes through bureaucratic rules and procedures. And the likely, indeed inevitable, longer term outcome of that process will be a closer fit between ability to pay and housing quality. As part of the general expansion of home ownership the broader consequence will be to produce a much clearer mosaic of housing inequalities associated with class and status differences within home ownership. In recent years a momentary and historically specific association between class and tenure (specifically council housing and sections of the working class) has confused analysts into seeing residential differentiation primarily in tenurial terms. With a majority of households increasingly in one tenure we are perhaps returning to a housing tenure profile reminiscent of the previous century when the vast majority were in private renting and tenure was marginal to analyses of inequality and stratification.

New times, new welfare states?

The title of this chapter reflects some of the grander claims made of rising home ownership and the role of council house sales in that growth. This view of the socially transformative effects of home ownership has a long history (see, for example, Pawley, 1978; Daunton 1987; Forrest et al., 1990) and the claim that it encourages thrift, stability, responsibility and other admirable qualities in citizens is regularly repeated. Implicit in many utterings of the Left and Right is the view that a million more home owners is a million less at the barricades. As Ward (1983) has observed, there is a

> .... fear that workers will be at home papering the parlour when they ought to be out on the streets making a revolution. (p. 186)

There is a strong belief that the growth of home ownership represents a more general social and cultural revolution. Such sentiments are well-expressed by John Stanley the first Minister of Housing and Construction under Thatcher.

I believe that no other single policy of our Government is bringing about a more profound, a more immediate and a more beneficial impact on the lives of hundreds of thousands of families in this country than the right to buy. And don't let anyone underestimate either the scale of the social revolution that is now taking place, or the determination of the Government to carry it further, and I mean a lot further. (Conservative Party Conference, 1982)

The sale of over a million dwellings to sitting tenants can however be seen as significant in a rather different way. Claims and counter claims about the impact of changing housing tenure on political consciousness or more recent sociological theorizing on the salience of divisions in social consumption can be set within a broader appreciation of the changed political economy. Sales of council dwellings can be seen as part of a progressive commodification of welfare provision which is in turn part and parcel of the search for new areas of profitable activity in capitalist societies. In such formulations consumer choice and preference is exercised within a logic circumscribed by the transformation of human needs and desires into commodities to be bought and sold in the market place. Such wordy Marxian terminology has become somewhat unfashionable in the housing literature but remains prominent within a broader literature concerned with the relationship between the state provision of goods and services and shifts in so-called regimes of accumulation and modes of regulation. Put crudely, it is argued that 'Fordism' is giving way to 'Post-Fordism', a regime of flexible as opposed to mass production, and that associated with those changes is the dismantling of the old collectivist Keynesian welfare-statism (e.g. King, 1989). This view is best summarized by Scott (1988) who states:

The forward surge of the new flexible production sectors at the core of the new regime of accumulation has been further underpinned by major changes in the mode of social regulation. There has been a wholesale dismantling of the apparatus of Keynesian welfare-statism and deepening privatisation of social life, a marked renewal of the forces of economic competition in industrial production and labour markets and (in the United States) a sharp rise in governmental allocations for the purchase of military and space equipment. These changes are still in many ways in an experimental stage and no doubt their full extent and form remain yet to be determined. (p. 175)

Both the basic formulation and the claimed consequences of these developments have met with a number of challenges (see, for example, Costello et al., 1989). And it remains the case that changes in the regime of accumulation have been rather more fully researched and articulated than the links between new spatial divisions of labour, changes in the production process, economic restructuring and contemporary welfare state forms. The connections between the sphere of production and post-Fordist forms of welfare provision are often only loosely made (though see Stoker, 1989). As Rustin (1989) observes

.... the kind of Fordist 'fit' between the mass production of goods and a similarly 'massified' provision of public services is taken as the model of

> the relation we should be looking for between flexible, consumer-led systems of production, and equally flexible, consumer-driven systems of welfare.

He goes on 'One implicit hypothesis is that consumers who are led to expect variety and choice in consumer markets will or should settle for nothing less in the welfare sector' (p. 59). In such a formulation deregulation and privatization of the welfare sector is delivering freedom, choice and reponsiveness to a disenfranchized public. However in Britain it is something of an overstatement to claim there has been a 'wholesale dismantling' of the post-war welfare state. Indeed, in more theoretically based discussions of the privatization of welfare under Thatcherism it is only state housing which emerges as the unambiguous example of recommodification. To what extent British council housing was ever decommodified remains contentious. After all, users paid a fee (rent) for a good produced by the private building industry financed by money raised on the private money market.

There are, however, a number of interrelated factors to take into account in seeking explanations for why mass sales of state dwellings occurred when they did and why state housing has borne the brunt of welfare state restructuring. These explanations operate at different levels of abstraction ranging from specific housing policy considerations to accounts which situate council house sales within a broader based view of welfare state restructuring on an international scale. Rather than rehearse these explanations in full it is appropriate to reflect on some of the accounts rooted in political economy which do connect processes of welfare state restructuring to shifts in modes of regulation in changing regimes of accumulation.

The promotion of mass home ownership has been at the centre of the political project of Thatcherism. And the sale of council housing has been a key mechanism in attempting to establish the hegemony of popular capitalism (Jessop, 1989). Not only did the policy deliver a 'stake in the system' with the assumed political pay-off that would entail but it also dismantled one of the key edifices of old style Labourism. It also delivered enormous capital receipts to a Treasury preoccupied with monetarist supply side economic policy (see Forrest and Murie, 1988a, for a more detailed account). Why is it that in Britain it is state housing rather than say health or education which has been so comprehensively reorganized? The simple answer is that the middle class do not use council housing and therefore there is no broad based political constituency to defend it. This can be expressed in different ways. In recent work Le Grand and Estrin (1989) following Titmuss and others (e.g. Titmuss, 1968), have shown that it is the middle classes who are the principal beneficiaries of the welfare state with the exception of council housing and housing benefits. And drawing on Korpi (1983), King (1989) refers to marginal and institutional forms of welfare provision and argues that it is the marginal form which is more likely to be eroded by right wing policies aimed at rolling back state provision. Institutional or universal forms of welfare such as the National Health Service or state education will have more broad based political support and their erosion will meet with greater political resistance. Moreover, with institutional forms there will be a much closer fit between the producers and users of the service. Hence, as with council housing, marginal forms of welfare provision are more likely to be services for a working class minority managed by a middle class professional bureaucracy. Whilst a professional group in this position may experience a threat to their job security they are less likely to mobilize in defence of the use values they are delivering. Much more likely is a paternalistic 'them and us' approach to service delivery. Such conceptions of forms of welfare provision and the political possibility of their reorganization have been taken further by Esping Andersen (1985). In a cross-national comparison of welfare states he argues that contrary to some conceptions it is not the case that New Right policies have been most effective in countries where decommodified forms have become most pervasive. On the contrary, it seems that the better established and more universalistic have been the social democratic forms of welfare provision, the less open they are to political challenge. Hence he argues that Britain and Denmark have seen more successful implementation of New Right policies than Norway or Sweden.

Another related perspective would emphasize the shifting position of the UK in the world economy. Such a perspective would emphasize the developing role of the UK as a centre for trans-national financial services and an associated weakening of the working class as skilled, unionized producers. Hence the strategic significance of the British working class shifts from being producers to be reproduced, to being consumers with an adequate credit base to reproduce themselves. And the political muscle of those outside the social consumption norms of the majority is seriously weakened by the diminished economic position of the unemployed or underemployed in a situation where not only are the production centres of capital situated elsewhere but consumer markets are increasingly global. Stated bluntly, in the past there was a strategic necessity to reproduce the necessary skilled labour power in particular locations. Becontree estate in Dagenham was quite literally a Fordist housing estate - high quality state housing for the skilled workers at the Ford factory. It is this same labour aristocracy who have benefited disproportionately from the Right to Buy and previous discretionary sales policies. Those next in the queue who would be the principal beneficiaries of new building in the state sector have neither the political representation (trade unionism) nor the economic muscle to demand a sustained high quality building programme. As Jessop (1989) remarks 'the neo-liberal social security state is discretionary, means tested and minimalist'. He goes on:

> .... the government is promoting popular capitalism as a substitute for the nanny state: housing owning, pension-owning, share owning and private medical insurance are subsidised through tax relief and are regarded as substitutes for council housing, adequate state pensions, income support and free health service. Where individuals and families cannot (or will not) make adequate private provision, a basic no frills state system will be provided, subject to rationing by queuing and/or involving minimalist,

revolving 'social funds' administered on a local, discretionary basis. (Jessop, p. 276)

What has happened to British council housing therefore can be set within a context of economic and labour market restructuring, the weakening and fragmentation of organized labour and within a developing ideological discourse where profit, the market, efficiency, value for money and the commodification of goods and services displace the language of equity, need and social justice. But such developments are neither inevitable nor universal (in many countries in Western Europe a social democratic discourse still dominates) and it is as well not to overstate explanations rooted in the logic of capitalism. Such accounts run the risk of functionalism and mono-causality. They are nevertheless important in providing a framework within which to situate processes of privatization and commodification and in countering voluntaristic, demand led explanations of social change. Moreover, in explaining why council housing rather than education or health has been extensively privatized in Britain one would have to acknowledge the important differences between housing and other state financed or state managed services. British council housing represented a massive, mature investment which could be realized through individual sale to the sole users. Moreover, the institutional and financial framework which had grown up around home ownership with a highly developed second hand market made privatization of state housing relatively unproblematic. In other countries with substantial public sectors but less developed private markets such a transfer of housing assets from the state to the private sector would be more complicated. And of course, a prerequisite to extensive housing privatization is a large, relatively high quality decommodified state housing sector accommodating a large number of working class households who are able and willing to purchase. It is for this reason that housing privatization is prominent in accounts of Thatcherite Britain and why there are few lessons in this context to transfer to, say, Japan or the USA. In the USA the skilled working classes in the primary labour markets were drawn much earlier into the majority tenure of home ownership. As Florida and Feldman observe in their discussion of 'Housing in US Fordism', 'The privileged position of the US in the global economy and the dynamics of the postwar accord allowed it to supplant social democratic Fordism with its own unique variant' (p. 203). In Britain the development of mass home ownership was rather slower and the extension of effective demand depended ultimately on the discounted sale of state dwellings. One perspective on the reorganization of housing provision which has occurred in the UK in recent years is that it is the owner occupied sector which has become increasingly socialized and subsidized. This process has extended and consolidated the regressive nature of welfare subsidies and the disproportionate benefits which accrue to the middle classes.

Moving columns and the excluded

Some contemporary accounts of the extension of home ownership (e.g. Saunders and Harris) invoke the image of a moving column whereby the privileges of the minority gradually filter down to the majority. The vast majority of households in Britain now own, for example, a range of consumer durables such as televisions, refrigerators, and washing machines. Car ownership is now enjoyed by the majority (although in this context it might be observed that the pace of movement of the column has slowed considerably). Saunders and Harris acknowledge the rather different circumstances which prevail in the housing market, particularly the problem of sufficiently lowering costs through productivity gains to increase effective demand. Nevertheless they claim that the growing middle mass of home owners 'literally share in the growing wealth of a capitalist economy and that they do in this sense have a very real stake in the system' (p. 33).

There is no question that the ownership of a dwelling can and does make a difference both as regards social status and material wealth. The question is how much of a difference it makes and whether housing tenure necessarily occupies the privileged position attributed to it by many commentators. To suggest that the extension of home ownership is delivering the positional advantages of the minority to the majority denies the very notion of positional goods - that they can only be enjoyed by a minority (Hirsch, 1977). As home ownership moves down the income structure so its positional status changes and it becomes highly differentiated and stratified. By the time the majority achieves the status of the minority, that group have moved on. In housing terms this may mean second homes abroad or the purchase of dwellings in hyper-inflating sub-markets in gentrifying inner urban locations or rural enclaves. And for the middle mass the experience is of widely differing housing market trajectories with capital gains and money accumulation which is highly differentiated socially and spatially. Despite Saunders and Harris's (1988) idiosyncratic calculations claiming to demonstrate that working class owners in general, and council house purchasers in particular, derive extraordinarily high rates of return from investment in home ownership they themselves acknowledge that 'The spread of home ownership thus reduces the relative inequality of wealth between more or less affluent groups, although the absolute gap between them is widened' (p. 29). The widening of the gap in absolute terms would seem to be a rather important counter to claims of a massive redistribution of wealth occurring with the spread of home ownership. Many of the questions can, however, really only be answered when housing wealth is realized and passed on to the next generation. Whether such transfers alter significantly existing patterns of wealth holding and, thus, class stratification, remains an empirical question. We have speculated elsewhere on some of the important dimensions to this process (Forrest and Murie, 1989) and empirical work by Hamnett et al. (1989) indicates the continuing salience of class position in housing wealth inheritance.

It remains to be seen therefore whether the sons and daughters of our early council house purchasers find themselves on a higher rung on the ladder. If they do, however, their privileged position will be because of, not despite, state housing. Their parents' stake in the system was delivered through state subsidy and state intervention in various forms at various times. Their housing histories and their attitudes towards state housing demonstrate their relatively protected position. There is certainly little indication of an experience of state housing which was damaging, paternalistic and repressive. It is important therefore to understand the position of those who have left the state sector not in a polarized way whereby their current status as home owners is contrasted starkly with their previous status as council tenants. Much of the current literature portrays this group as escaping from a tenure form which stifled their aspirations and inhibited their freedom and independence. It would be more accurate to describe their previous status as tenants as a precondition for their current housing location.

The imagery of a moving column needs to be modified in a further way. Many people will not form part of any of the columns of home owners. Indeed, once the moving columns have passed by, the housing resources available to them will be diminished. The evidence presented in this book on council housing after privatization is that it ceases to be available to the homeless, those with lowest incomes and those with least bargaining power. What happens to these groups depends on two factors. First, social, economic and demographic trends will determine the size, distribution and nature of these groups. Secondly, the supply of housing will determine what is available to them. At present the scenario for these groups is not an optimistic one. Recent social trends indicate growing numbers of people dependent on welfare benefits or incomes below that which is necessary to obtain housing in the market. At the same time the supply of high quality, social rented housing is in decline. What is filtering down to this section of the community is not the privileges of the minority but rather a greater exposure to homelessness and bad housing, and less opportunity to become part of the moving column through access to council housing.

Concluding Comments

It has been acknowledged elsewhere that the former tenants in this study cannot be claimed to be typical or representative of those purchasing today. Nevertheless, their attitudes and experiences can be set against some of the generalizations in the literature about privatization. We might have a number of expectations of this group of households. They would have bought to escape from a council sector which they found to be highly unsatisfactory. They would have moved relatively quickly to embark on a conscious investment strategy in the owner occupied market and to enhance their social status. Their life chances and material situation would by now have been dramatically transformed through tenure change and the opportunity to buy. None of this is borne out by the evidence from this study. If anything the picture is of relative continuity and stability - of a group who in the main would by now have been very affluent tenants. Some have moved on but there is no strong evidence of conscious housing investment strategies. Some have fared rather better than others. Some have substantial savings, many have generous occupational pensions and a number have received substantial redundancy payments. Where households have moved, job reasons have been important. Their material circumstances as tenants and owners are more closely connected to their position in the labour market than their status as home owners. Many analysts overprivilege house tenure in their accounts of contemporary social change and confuse effect with cause. There is a need to calm the current excitement about the impact of mass sales and extended home ownership. The role and status of British social housing have been dramatically transformed in the last decade and it has been pushed further towards the minimal or marginal model of state welfare. A decade from now that may be the most enduring effect of the social revolution. The post revolutionary development of home ownership will display greater fragmentation and differentiation. Rather than one moving column it will be evident that there are a large number of different queues moving at varying paces in varying directions. The group of households in this study were in one column shaped by a particular set of historical and policy circumstances. Other tenants at that time took a quite different route and bought elsewhere in the private sector. And for those waiting to enter, the routes they will take are likely to be distinctly different. Rather glib remarks that 'The challenge for the 1990s is how to extend these benefits [capital accumulation through housing] to the tenants who remain' (Saunders and Harris, 1988, p. 25) betray a vision of a benevolent capitalism responding to consumer demand. After this phase of privatization these benefits could be delivered by embarking on a large scale public sector building programme (albeit much more responsive to consumer preferences) and selling them to the new tenants at a substantial discount. Instead such a policy is portrayed as wasteful and profligate and an increasingly marginalized minority is offered a new breed of landlords. Substantial tenant resistance to such transfers underlines the view that 'exiting' from the public sector is related to the destination on offer and the incentives involved. Crude generalizations about dissatisfaction with public housing and the unpopularity of collective provision are only that.

State housing after privatization fits into a highly stratified and fragmented home ownership market. Here, post-Fordist images abound - life styles, market segmentation, market niche. Those who leave the state housing sector join the ranks of a majority where self-realization is achieved supposedly through the act of consuming and where the owned home is central to that process as regards social status and credit rating. But such a perspective understates the whole range of other influences which shape people's lives - including the world of work, financial resources, family and kinship ties, life cycle stage and attachment to particular neighbourhoods.

Finally, this research indicates the need for caution in accepting too readily the association between extending market processes and achieving more equitable and responsive housing provision. Liberal theorists concerned with distributional issues embrace the ideology of consumerism and market processes as if material acquisition through fairer competition could more successfully achieve some of the greater humanitarian ideals which remain an important part of the history of public housing. This view tends to neglect issues of supply and the contribution of council housing in producing and continuing to provide what consumers wanted and in allocating it to people who could not have obtained it through market processes. Moreover, much of the discourse of involvement and participation as active consumers through market processes is highly elitist and neglects aspects of power and powerlessness. It also neglects the reality of an underclass excluded from the social consumption norms of the majority through low earning and dwindling state benefits. Whilst the nature and significance of this underclass remains undertheorized, their deteriorating social and economic position is more likely to be exacerbated by the extension of market processes.

Appendix: notes on method

As we have stressed in the main body of the text, one of the key aims of the research was to investigate the housing destinations of sitting tenant purchasers who had subsequently sold their former council house and moved on. There are various questions related to issues of social and spatial mobility which are relevant in this context. The tracing of moving households is, however, a difficult endeavour and this element of the research was always regarded as exploratory. Problems of tracing are increased in a situation where moves may have occurred at any time over the last fifteen or twenty years.

In the research design our principal strategy for tracing movers was straightforward. In the main survey stage (stage 1) questionnaires were colour coded - white for an original council house purchaser (OCHP) and green for households who had moved into the estate when the property had been resold (NOCHP) on the open market. The green questionnaires contained a series of questions attempting to determine

(a) whether the previous owner had bought as a sitting tenant

(b) where they had moved to.

They would then generate a number of follow-up addresses for stage 2 interviews. At the end of stage 1 the overall position was as follows:

	London	Birmingham	All
White (OCHP)	112	134	246
Green (NOCHP)	85	82	167
Pink (successor)	2	3	5
	199	219	418

The tracer sections on the green questionnaire generated the following information for follow-up interviews:

Tracer Address	London	Birmingham	All
Full	5	11	16
Partial	5	9	14
Limited	33	22	55
No address	42	40	82
Total Green (NOCHP)	85	82	167

There were 85 addresses where some information was available, but only 16 where a full tracer address was available. This was disappointing, although not necessarily surprising. If some time has elapsed since a move occurred, households are unlikely to have retained a forwarding address. There is also understandable reluctance to offer information about other households. Moreover, even when an address (full or partial) was obtained there was no guarantee that the OCHP had not moved subsequently and that the contact address would not now be occupied by a different household.

Because of the limited information on tracer addresses obtained from the social survey, other methods of tracing were investigated. Some consideration was given to the NHS Central Register located at Southport which has been used to examine patterns of mobility and migration. The DSS central register at Newcastle-upon-Tyne was an alternative. Using either source raises problems of confidentiality and can be extremely time consuming to attempt to trace individuals (rather than establish broad patterns). The main constraint we faced, however, concerned the data required for tracing. Ideally, National Insurance numbers were required for tracing through DSS. It was possible to use date of birth, although this was less assured of success. We explored the use of DSS records as a tracing method on more limited data by calculating the approximate date of birth (i.e. year) from the information available from the original survey of Birmingham purchasers carried out in 1973. The procedure for DSS tracing was to fill in a separate form for each trace (details of surname, initials, last known address and approximate age). A small charge was made for each trace. To preserve confidentiality any successful traces would be contacted to seek co-operation by letter sent via the DSS. Unfortunately, our limited data proved inadequate for tracing purposes (an actual date of birth was required as minimum information) and we were forced to abandon this method.

Subsequently, further effort was made to follow up the information obtained in the social survey through using telephone directories. The survey had generated 120 names for telephone tracing. There were 85 (43 London, 42 Birmingham) for which some tracer information was available. Secondly, there were the 35 Birmingham OCHP names which were either different from the tracer name or where there was no tracer name, and where the OCHP name was judged to be not too 'common' (e.g. F. Smith would yield too many possible telephone numbers).

This part of the tracing was carried out primarily by On-Line, MORI's telephone research subsidiary, using the same regional telephone directories to find all the possible telephone numbers for each tracer name and address. This telephone number tracing on 120 names gave the following results:

	Tracer Names
None*	28
1	30
2-5	15
6-10	16
11-20	8
21+	23
Total	120

* including those where tracer letters were sent - see below.

Telephone interviews

It was decided to attempt to contact by telephone all those with between one and ten possible telephone numbers - 61 names. This part of the work was carried out by an experienced MORI interviewer working at different times and days, including evenings and weekends.

The first part of the telephone interviewing was to 'filter' for the correct telephone number - i.e. given the household tracer name, had they ever lived at the OCHP address. Secondly, if they had lived there, were they OCHPs? If they were not, then a short telephone interview should be completed; if they were the OCHP, then they should be asked to agree to the full face to face interview.

The results were:

	Tracer Names
Wrong household(s)	39
No contact	5
Not OCHP/short interview (including 1 unconfirmed follow-up)	7
OCHP/full interview	
- agreed	8
- refused	2
Total	61

Letter tracing

In addition to tracing by telephone, an attempt was also made to contact by letter where (some) address was available, but no telephone number had been found. The letter included an appropriate self-completion questionnaire (specifying the OCHP address and OCHP in Birmingham) and reply-paid envelope to MORI. Thirteen letters were initially despatched, plus five repeat reminder letters sent a few weeks later. In addition, as follow-ups to replies were received, two further tracer letters plus questionnaire were despatched.

In summary:

	Tracer Names
Returned	
- incomplete address	3
- gone away	2
No reply	2
Replied	
- bought from OCHP	3
(including 2 for follow-up)	
- did not buy from OCHP	1
- OCHP from original letters	2
(plus follow-up confirmed	1)
Total	13

Full interviewing

Taking together contacts made by telephone and letter, twelve OCHP full interviews were issued (nine telephone tracing/three tracer letters; nine Birmingham/three London). This included one unconfirmed follow-up address from the telephone tracing. Interviewers were asked to seek the respondent's co-operation in taping the interview.

The outcome on interviews completed and taped was:

	OCHP
Completed	9
(of which taped	4)
Refused	1
Family illness/postponed	1
Unconfirmed/moved away	1
Total	12

Bibliography

Advertising Service Guild (1943) *An Enquiry into People's Homes* London: John Murray.

BMRB (1986) *Housing and Savings* London: Building Societies Association.

BMRB (1989) *Housing and Savings* London: Building Societies Association.

Bournville Village Trust (1941) *When We Build Again* London: George Allen and Unwin.

Building Societies Association (1983) *Housing Tenure* London: BSA.

Building Societies Association (1989) *Housing in Britain* London: BSA.

Centre for Housing Research (1989) *The Nature and Effectiveness of Housing Management in England,* London: HMSO.

City of Peterborough (1986) *Market Survey*: Attitude of tenants in Peterborough Development Corporation residential properties to transfer of ownership.

City of Peterborough (1987) *Housing Transfer Tenant consultations*: Results.

Clinton, A., Murie, A., Paice, D., Tolan, F., and Williams, P. (1989) *The Relative Effectiveness of Different Forms of Housing Management in Wales,* unpublished report to Welsh Office.

Costello, N., Michie, J. and Milne, S. (1989) *Beyond the Casino Economy* London: Verso.

Cullingworth, J.B. (1963) *Housing in Transition* London: Heinemann.

Daunton, M. (1987) *A Property Owning Democracy?* London: Freedom Press.

Department of the Environment (1977) *Housing Policy: Technical Volume, Part I* London: HMSO.

Department of the Environment (1978) *National Dwelling and Housing Survey*, London: HMSO.
Department of the Environment (1986) *English House Condition Survey 1986*, London: HMSO.
Esping Andersen, G. (1985) 'Power and Distributional Regimes' *Politics and Society* 4: 223-56.
Florida, R.L. and Feldman, M. (1988) 'Housing in US Fordism' *International Journal of Urban and Regional Research* Vol. 12, 187-210.
Forrest, R. (1980) 'The Resale of Former Council Housing in Birmingham' *Policy and Politics* Vol. 8: 3.
Forrest, R. (1983) 'The Meaning of Home Ownership' Environment and Planning D: Society and Space, Vol. 1: 2.
Forrest, R., Lansley, S. and Murie, A. (1984) *A Foot on the Ladder?* Working Paper No. 41, School for Advanced Urban Studies, University of Bristol.
Forrest, R. and Murie, A. (1976) *Social Segregation, housing need and the sale of council houses*, Research Memorandum 53, University of Birmingham: Centre for Urban and Regional Research.
Forrest, R. and Murie, A. (1982) *Council House Sales and Council Housing in Birmingham* Unpublished research report, Centre for Urban and Regional Research, University of Birmingham.
Forrest, R. and Murie, A. (1984) *Monitoring the Right to Buy*, Working Paper No. 41, University of Bristol: School for Advanced Urban Studies.
Forrest, R. and Murie, A. (1985) *Housing Origins and Destinations*, end of award report, Grant No. DUU23/2033, ESRC.
Forrest, R. and Murie, A. (1987) 'The Affluent Home Owner: labour market position and the shaping of housing histories' *Sociological Review* Vol. 35: 2, 370-403.
Forrest, R. and Murie, A. (1988a) *Selling the Welfare State* London: Routledge.
Forrest, R. and Murie, A. (1988b) 'Putting Trust in Tenants' *Municipal Journal*, 22 January, p. 98.
Forrest, R. and Murie, A. (1989) 'Differential Accumulation: Wealth, inheritance and housing policy reconsidered' *Policy and Politics* Vol. 17: 1.
Forrest, R., Murie, A. and Williams, P. (1990) *Home Ownership: Differentiation and Fragmentation* London: Unwin Hyman.
Foulis, M.B. (1985) *Council House Sales in Scotland* Scottish Office: Central Research Unit.
Franklin, A. (1989) 'Working Class Privatism: an historical case study of Bedminster, Bristol', *Environment and Planning D: Society and Space*, Vol. 7, 93-113.
Gallup (1988) *Council Tenants*: Research on behalf of National Consumer Council, London: Gallup.
Garrahan, P. (1977) 'Housing, The Class Milieu and Middle Class Conservatism' *British Journal of Political Science*, Vol. 7, 125-6.
Gray, F. (1982) 'Owner occupation and social relations' in Merrett, S. with Gray, F. *Owner Occupation in Britain* London: Routledge and Kegan Paul.

Greater London Council (1976) *Home Sweet Home* London: Academy Editions.

Haddon, R. (1970) 'A minority in a welfare state society', *New Atlantis*, 2, 80-133.

Hamnett, C. and Randolph, B. (1988) *Cities, Housing and Profits* London: Hutchinson.

Hamnett, C., Harmer, M. and Williams, P. (1989) *Housing Inheritance: A national survey of its scale and impact* London: Housing Research Foundation.

Harvey, D. (1989) *The Urban Experience* Oxford: Blackwell.

Heath, A., Jowell, R. and Curtice, J. (1985) *How Britain Votes* Oxford: Pergamon Press.

Hirsch, F. (1977) *Social Limits to Growth* London: Routledge and Kegan Paul.

Hooimeijer, P. and Linde, M. (1988) *Vergrijzing, Individualisering en de Woningmarkt,* Utrecht: Drukkerij Elinkwijk BV.

Jessop, B. (1989) 'Conservative Regimes and the Transition to Post-Fordism: The Cases of Great Britain and West Germany' in Gottdiener, N. and Komninos, N. (eds) *Capitalist Development and Crisis Theory: Accumulation, Regulation and Spatial Restructuring* London: Macmillan.

Johnston, R.J. (1987) 'A note on housing tenure and voting in Britain 1983' *Housing Studies*, Vol. 2: 2, 112-121.

Jowell, R. and Airey, C. (1984) *British Social Attitudes: the 1984 Report,* Aldershot: Gower.

Jowell, R., Witherspoon, S. and Brook, L. (1986) *British Social Attitudes: the 1986 report* Aldershot: Gower.

Kerr, M. (1988) *The Right to Buy* Department of the Environment, HMSO.

King, D. (1989) 'Economic Crisis and Welfare State Recommodification: A Comparative Analysis of the United States and Britain' in Gottdiener, M. and Komninos, N. (eds) *Capitalist Development and Crisis Theory: Accumulation, Regulation and Spatial Restructuring* London: Macmillan.

Korpi, W. (1983) *The Democratic Class Struggle* London: Routledge and Kegan Paul.

Le Grand, J. and Estrin, S. (eds) (1989) *Market Socialism,* Oxford: Clarendon Press.

London Housing News (1988) 'Thamesmead Residents want local authority landlord', April, pp 1-2.

Marshall, G., Newby, H., Rose, D. and Kogler, C. (1988) *Social Class in Modern Britain* London: Hutchinson.

McCulloch, A. (1989) 'A Millstone Round your Neck: Building Societies in the 1930s and Mortgage Default' *Housing Studies*, Vol. 5.1.

Merrett, S. with Gray, F. (1982) *Owner Occupation in Britain* London: Routledge and Kegan Paul.

MORI (1988) *Manchester Residents Housing*, April, Research conducted for Manchester City Council.

Murie, A. (1975) *The Sale of Council Houses: A study in social policy,* Occasional Paper No. 35, University of Birmingham: Centre for Urban and Regional Research.

Murie, A. (1986) 'Social differentiation in urban areas: housing or occupational class at work?' *Tijdscrift voor Economische en Social Geografie*, 77, 345-57.

Murie, A. (1990) 'Divisions of Home Ownership: Housing Tenure and Social Change' *Environment and Planning A*, forthcoming.

Murie, A., Niner, P. and Watson, C. (1976) *Housing Policy and the Housing System* London: Allen and Unwin.

Northern Ireland Housing Executive (1981) *House Sales Programme: Household Survey - Survey Report*, Corporate Planning Department, NIHE, Belfast.

OPCS (1986) *General Household Survey 1984* London: HMSO.

OPCS (1989) *General Household Survey 1987* London: HMSO.

Pahl, R.E. (1975) *Whose City?* Harmondsworth: Penguin, Second Edition.

Pahl, R.E. and Wallace, C.D. (1988) 'Neither angels in marble nor rebels in red: privatization and working class consciousness' in Rose, D. (ed.) *Social Stratification and Economic Change* London: Hutchinson.

Pawley, M. (1978) *Home Ownership* London: Architectural Press.

Pratt, G. (1982) 'Class analysis and urban domestic property' *International Journal of Urban and Regional Research*, Vol. 6, 481-502.

Prescott-Clarke, P., Allen, P. and Morrissey, C. (1988) *Queuing for Housing: a study of council house waiting lists* London: HMSO.

Rex, J. and Moore, R. (1967) *Race, Community and Conflict* Oxford: Oxford University Press.

Rossi, H. (1977) 'Adding to the stock of human happiness' *Roof*, 12.

Runciman, W.G. (1966) *Relative Deprivation and Social Justice*, London: Routledge and Kegan Paul.

Rustin, M. (1989) 'The Shape of New Times' *New Left Review* 175, 54-77.

Saunders, P. (1986) *Social Theory and the Urban Question*, Second Edition, London: Hutchinson.

Saunders, P. (1990) *A Nation of Home Owners* London: Unwin Hyman.

Saunders, P. and Harris, C. (1987) 'Biting the Nipple? Consumers, Preferences and State Welfare' Paper presented at the Sixth Urban Change and Conflict Conference, University of Kent, September 20-23.

Saunders, P. and Harris, C. (1988) *Home Ownership and Capital Gains* University of Sussex: Urban and Regional Studies, Working Paper 64.

Saunders, P. and Williams, P. (1988) 'The Constitution of the Home: Towards a Research Agenda' *Housing Studies* Vol. 3: 2, 81-93.

Scott, A. (1988) 'Flexible production systems and regional development: the rise of new industrial space in North America and western Europe' *International Journal of Urban and Regional Research* Vol. 12: 2, 171-186.

Sewel, J., Twine, F. and Williams, N. (1984) 'The sale of council houses - some empirical evidence' *Urban Studies* Vol. 21, 439-50.

Smith, N. and Williams, P. (1986) *Gentrification and the City* London: Allen and Unwin.

Stoker, G. (1989) 'Restructuring local government for a post-Fordist society?' Paper given at Urban Change and Conflict Conference, University of Bristol, 17-20 September.

Sullivan, O. (1989) 'Housing tenure as a consumption-sector divide: a critical perspective' *International Journal of Urban and Regional Research* Vol. 13, 183-200.

Taylor-Gooby, P. (1985) *Ideology, Public Opinion and Social Welfare* London: Routledge and Kegan Paul.

Titmuss, R. (1968) *Commitment to Welfare* London: Allen and Unwin.

Ward, C. (1983) *Housing: An Anarchist Approach* London: Freedom Press.

Index of authors